D0880960

THE GREAT HISPANIC HERITAGE

Frida Kahlo

Second Edition

THE GREAT HISPANIC HERITAGE

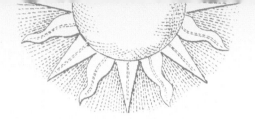

THE GREAT HISPANIC HERITAGE

Frida Kahlo
Second Edition

John Morrison and Jamie Pietras

CHELSEA HOUSE
PUBLISHERS
An imprint of Infobase Publishing

Frida Kahlo, Second Edition
Copyright © 2010 by Infobase Publishing

Chelsea House
An imprint of Infobase Publishing
132 West 31st Street
New York NY 10001

Library of Congress Cataloging-in-Publication Data
Pietras, Jamie.
  Frida Kahlo / Jamie Pietras. — 2nd ed.
    p. cm. — (Great Hispanic heritage)
  Rev. ed. of: Frida Kahlo / John Morrison. 2003.
  Includes bibliographical references and index.
  ISBN 978-1-60413-846-7 (hardcover)
  1. Kahlo, Frida—Juvenile literature. 2. Painters—Mexico—Biography—Juvenile literature. I. Kahlo, Frida. II. Morrison, John, 1929– Frida Kahlo. III. Title. IV. Series.
  ND259.K33M67 2011
  759.972—dc22
  [B]   2010009489

Text design by Terry Mallon
Cover design by Terry Mallon/Alicia Post
Composition by EJB Publishing Services
Cover printed by Bang Printing, Brainerd, MN
Book printed and bound by Bang Printing, Brainerd, MN
Date printed: September 2010
Printed in the United States of America

10 9 8 7 6 5 4 3 2 1

This book is printed on acid-free paper.

Contents

The Unconquerable Spirit

Frida Kahlo nearly died that day, and the world would have been denied the pleasure and stimulation of viewing the dramatic and haunting paintings of one of Mexico's most heralded artists. In fact, it could be argued that the accident, as horrific as it was, made Kahlo the artist that she became. But at that moment on September 17, 1925, there was only pain and terror.

THE ACCIDENT

It was one of those flukes of fate that change a life forever. The bus was a new model, made of wood and brightly painted, with rows of seats facing each other. The 18-year-old schoolgirl and her boyfriend shouldn't have been on that bus in the first place. They intended to take another bus for the ride to their home in Coyoacán, outside Mexico City. But Frida Kahlo discovered that a toy parasol that her friend,

Alejandro Gómez Arias, had bought her during the day's shopping trip was missing.

The two retraced their steps, searching for the parasol. When they couldn't find it, they bought a balero, which is a cup-and-ball toy. Then they spotted the other bus and decided to take it home. In fact, they felt lucky that the vehicle came along when it did.

The bus driver made a critical mistake when he crossed at an intersection in the path of an electric streetcar. The trolley rammed the side of the bus and kept pushing the other vehicle until it was wedged against a wall. The heavier trolley continued to apply pressure on the bus until the wooden vehicle virtually exploded into splinters.

Gómez Arias was knocked unconscious and thrown out of the bus. When he came to, he was under the streetcar and his clothing had been shredded. The trolley was still moving, and he was sure he would be crushed. But the car finally stopped, and he was able to crawl out from under it. He hurried to the smashed bus to find Kahlo. He managed to work his way inside and was greeted by a horrifying sight. A metal handrail had rammed through Kahlo's body. Her clothing had been ripped away. She lay there naked, bleeding, and, strangely, covered with a fine coating of gold dust that a fellow passenger, a house painter, had been carrying in a bag. A woman passenger thought she looked like a dancer and exclaimed, "Help for the little ballerina!"

Kahlo was so stunned that she didn't realize what had happened to her. She later wrote that her first thought was to look for the balero. "I did not assess the situation nor did I guess the kind of wounds I had," she wrote.

Gómez Arias started to pick Kahlo up to get her out of the wreckage, but she shrieked in pain. A man nearby said, "We have to take it out," speaking of the metal rod. He put a knee on her body and pulled the rod out of her. Gómez Arias said later that her screams were louder than the sirens of the

In this painting, Frida Kahlo depicts the horrifying streetcar accident in which she was involved at the age of 18. The accident inflicted emotional wounds that lingered long after her physical wounds healed. Kahlo harnessed that pain to create some of the world's most haunting paintings.

ambulances that arrived. She was taken to the Red Cross Hospital and at first was placed among the more severely injured, whom the doctors thought could not be saved. But Gómez Arias pleaded with them to work on her, and she underwent the first of many operations that marked the course of her painful life. It was up to the medical community to put Kahlo's shattered body back together again.

Her spinal column was broken in three places in the lumbar region. Her collarbone and her third and fourth ribs were broken. Kahlo's right leg had 11 fractures, and her right foot was dislocated and crushed. Her left shoulder was out of joint, her pelvis broken in three places.

Kahlo always maintained that the metal rod that entered through her left hip exited through her vagina, damaging her uterus and rendering her incapable of bearing children.

"I lost my virginity," she said. Gómez Arias said the wound was higher in the abdomen and maintained that Kahlo had, not uncharacteristically, invented the site of the exit. It was a lifelong habit of Kahlo's to embellish experiences for dramatic effect.

Regardless, the accident had turned a high-spirited, happy schoolgirl, who loved to run and dance, to tease and joke, into a rigid, grim creature immobilized and enclosed in plaster casts and other devices and suffering constant pain.

"In this hospital," she told Gómez Arias, "death dances around my bed."

KAHLO BEGINS TO PAINT

As horrible as the accident was, it induced Kahlo to start painting as a form of therapy. Her mother rigged up a mirror on Frida's four-poster bed so she could paint while lying down. Although she had been drawing and sketching since childhood and had studied art and composition in school, it was during her convalescence from the accident that she began seriously to try to put to canvas not only her personal visions, but the powerful feelings she had for the people and vistas of her native land.

Today, the work of Frida Kahlo is known around the world. In her short life—she died at 47—she produced some 200 paintings. Most were self-portraits—strong, vibrant pictures with colors as hot as the Mexican sun, celebrating the people, flora (plant life), and landscapes of Mexico, and full of the passionate intensity of life that still surged throughout her body, unhealthy as she felt it may have been. As the French author J.M.G. Le Clézio once put it: "Art, childhood, beauty, violence and love were indissolubly linked in the luxury she conjured up around her . . ."

Actually, it took a long time for Kahlo to be recognized as an artist in her own right because for years she lived in the shadow of her husband, the great muralist Diego Rivera. During her lifetime, she deferred to him as the "master"—

master not only of their home, but also of the art they each created.

Rivera and Kahlo were certainly the odd couple of the art world. His paintings were immense, typically covering entire walls; hers were small, often no more that two feet square (.185 square meters). He was huge, over six feet tall (183 centimeters), at times weighing as much as 300 pounds (136 kilograms); she was petite, five feet three inches (160 cm) and rarely weighing as much as 100 pounds (45 kg). And, at 43, he was 20 years older than her when they were married. Kahlo was darkly attractive, given to colorful costumes and flamboyant jewelry that drew all eyes to her on the street. Rivera was drab and homely, with a huge head, a blubbery face, and bulging eyes atop a bloated body.

Despite their differences, the couple shared a kind of magnetism that drew others into their sphere. Both had numerous romances, before and during their two marriages, which caused raging battles and long separations. When the fights and betrayals went beyond endurance, they divorced, only to remarry a year later. It seemed they could neither live with nor without each other.

During their heyday in the 1920s and 1930s, Frida Kahlo and Diego Rivera met and mixed with some of the era's most prominent individuals: fellow artists, politicians, movie stars, and the world's rich and famous. Their doings were duly reported in the press, and they were seen as glamorous figures.

Both Kahlo and Rivera were dedicated to the principles of the Mexican Revolution of 1910, and both celebrated the revolutionary spirit in their art. Kahlo even tried to change the date of her birth from 1907 to 1910, when leaders like Emiliano Zapata, Pancho Villa, and Francisco Madero began the struggle that would end the repressive 35-year regime of President Porfirio Díaz and transform the nation.

In a way, her afflictions paralleled those of her native land, torn and troubled for centuries by foreign invaders, corrupt officials, and brutal wars. But, like the spirit of

Mexico, Kahlo's spirit was never seriously squelched. She might have been puzzled at how, years after her death, she has become something of a feminist icon. Kahlo fans are inspired by the life of a woman who, though married to a strong,

In 2001, The U.S. Postal Service commemorated Kahlo's contribution to art with a stamp bearing her image. The first stamp honoring a Hispanic woman, it sealed Kahlo's status as a major presence for people of Hispanic heritage.

KAHLO LIVES ON

Frida Kahlo is admired globally for her undying spirit and unique vision. The pop singer Madonna, herself strongly individualistic and independent, owns two of Kahlo's paintings. Madonna said she identifies with the artist's "pain and her sadness." Kahlo's work has been shown at exhibits around the world to great critical acclaim. In 2001, the U.S. Postal Service issued a 34-cent stamp of her 1933 *Self-portrait with a Necklace*. One of her paintings was in the Metropolitan Museum of Art's surrealism exhibit (although Kahlo herself probably would have objected to being classified as a surrealist), while another sold for more than $5 million at auction.

A movie has been made of Frida Kahlo's life, with Salma Hayek starring in the lead role. Many books, including a novel, have been written about her. There has even been a traveling exhibit of photographs featuring Kahlo. She was on the cover of *Time* magazine; Volvo used her image to sell cars to Hispanics. Her typically unsmiling, dark-browed visage can be found on posters, T-shirts, calendars, and many other objects. Over the years, there have been Kahlo look-alike contests, and Kahlo operas, plays, documentaries, and even a cookbook. Frida Kahlo's former home in Coyoacán is now a museum and one of Mexico's great tourist attractions. A Frida Kahlo exhibition held at Mexico City's the Fine Arts Palace in the summer of 2007 was wildly successful, breaking the museum's attendance record.

domineering man, still managed to do her own remarkable work and keep her independent spirit.

What is it about this woman, crippled from the age of six by polio, smashed and broken in a horrendous street accident, not conventionally pretty, a heavy smoker and drinker, a dedicated Communist, abused and betrayed by both life and lovers, that has made her a heroine for many yearning souls and a figure of almost mythic proportions?

It was not only her remarkable talent as a painter and skill at producing art that for many people resonates so deeply. There was also her indomitable spirit and love of life, characteristics that all the pain and disappointments she endured could not diminish. That spirit she carried to the end. In 1953, after her right leg had been amputated below the knee because of gangrene, she wrote in her diary: "Pies para qué los quiero, si tengo alas pa' volar?" (Feet, why do I want them if I have wings to fly?)

One of her last paintings is a still life of ripe watermelons, inscribed with the words, "Viva la vida"—Long live life.

The Serious One

There she is in family photographs, the dark one, scowling at the camera. In some pictures, she is dressed in a man's suit. Even photographed as a child, with a sister and a girlfriend in a formal studio setting, she is the serious one; the others radiate innocence. And yet, by all accounts, Frida Kahlo had a good childhood. Even after she was afflicted with polio at the age of six and left with a deformed right leg, she exhibited a spirit that was at times ungovernable.

For years, scholars believed Kahlo's father, Carl Wilhelm Kahlo, was a Jew of Hungarian descent. More recent research suggests he descended from a line of Germans who were Lutheran. Having moved to Mexico in 1891, Carl Wilhelm changed his forename to Guillermo and within a few years married his first wife, with whom he had two daughters. Guillermo Kahlo was slender and handsome, with a giant bushy moustache and dark, piercing eyes. After his first wife died while giving birth to their second daughter, Guillermo married Matilde Calderón, a woman he met working at a jewelry store in Mexico City. Calderón was also stunning, with high cheekbones and delicate features. Of the four children he had with his second wife, he was most fond of Frida, born Magdalena Carmen Frida Kahlo y Calderón on July 6, 1907. He called her his "Liebe Frida" (Darling Frida) and pampered her greatly, especially after her bout with polio.

"Frida is my most intelligent daughter," he said. "She's most like me."

Frida wasn't much like her mother when it came to matters of faith. Matilde Calderón was a devout Catholic who took her religion to the point of bigotry, and this was a major factor in turning Frida against organized religion at an early age. Though Frida's first two given names were Christian, it was her third name—*Frieda*, as she spelled it until the late 1930s, when the Nazis ascended to power in Germany—by which she came to be known. In German, the name translated to the word "peace."

She was born at the Casa Azul (Blue House) on Allende Street in the village of Coyoacán, a southern suburb of Mexico City. Her father had built the home in 1904. Originally painted white, it was a one-story, U-shaped building with an inner court filled with subtropical plants. Inspired by Mexican artistic traditions, Kahlo and Diego Rivera later decided to give it its cheerful blue makeover.

Kahlo and Rivera would live in the house for many years, and after her death, Rivera had it enlarged and turned into a museum dedicated to Kahlo's work and Mexican culture. Kahlo immortalized the house in a painting, *My Grandparents, My Parents and I,* in 1936.

Frida's mother, Matilde Calderón, must have been a difficult woman. She refused to raise her husband's two daughters from his first marriage and had them sent to a convent orphanage. She was sickly, especially after her last daughter, Cristina, was born just 11 months after Frida's birth, and

Kahlo and her sister pose near their home. Kahlo had three sisters and two half-sisters. She often remarked that she grew up surrounded by females, although her father was a great influence on her.

she sought solace in the Catholic Church. More than likely, Matilde was depressed. Her sadness was probably explained, in part, by the leather-bound book Frida recalled having seen in her mother's possession. The book contained letters written to her mother by a young German man with whom she'd fallen in love before she met her husband. Tragically, that early romance ended with the man committing suicide in front of Matilde.

"My mother was excessively religious," Kahlo once said. "We had grace before every meal and, while the others were concentrating on their inner selves, Crist [her sister] and I would just look at one another and choke back our laughter." Likewise, when Frida and Cristina were supposed to attend a class to prepare them for their First Holy Communion, the two instead hid in a nearby orchard, eating "haws, quinces and capulines [a fruit similar to cherries]," according to recollections in Kahlo's journal. Kahlo had mixed emotions

MY GRANDPARENTS, MY PARENTS AND I

My Grandparents, My Parents and I is an exploration of identity, depicting Kahlo as a young girl of about two years of age, standing naked in the courtyard holding a ribbon that extends to images of her grandparents in the clouds. Guillermo and Matilde appear directly above her, looking not much different than they did in their wedding photo—right down to the ruffles and bows in Matilde's dress and Guillermo's small boutonniere. The artificial clouds that appear in the couple's wedding portrait are the likely inspiration for Kahlo's use of cloud imagery in her 1936 painting. Interestingly, Kahlo's maternal grandmother is shown to share her defining physical characteristic: the thick eyebrows she featured in so many of her self-portraits. This was not the case in real life. Kahlo exaggerated this feature in her grandmother for the sake of the piece.

regarding her mother, alternately referring to her in an interview as "cruel" and "very nice, active intelligent."

While Matilde Calderón encouraged her children's religious development, the streets of Mexico City taught Kahlo some grim lessons in early twentieth-century Mexican politics. From the time dictator Porfirio Díaz was overthrown in May 1911, various factions had been struggling to gain political power in the country. Violence was not uncommon. Writing in her diary, Kahlo recalled having witnessed gun battles between peasant followers of Emiliano Zapata (Zapatistas) and the followers of Venustiano Carranza (Carrancistas) during the "tragic ten days" battle in February 1913. Kahlo recounted her mother having opened her windows on Allende Street: "She gave access to the Zapatistas, seeing to it that the wounded and hungry jumped from the windows of my house into the living room," Kahlo wrote. "She cured them and gave them thick tortillas, the only food that could be obtained in Coyoacán in those days." If Frida Kahlo's memories hold true (a prominent Kahlo biographer,

FAMOUS CONTEMPORÁNEOS

During her time at the National Preparatory School, Kahlo got to know some of the country's burgeoning literary talent. The openly gay writer Salvador Novo, for example, was active in the Contemporáneos clique before going on to become a poet, playwright, and official chronicler of Mexico City. The poet Carlos Pellicer was a Contemporáneos member and a good friend of Kahlo (and later Rivera); he was known, early in his career, for his evocative depictions of landscapes. Xavier Villaurrutia, meanwhile, left a legacy of short dramas and poems that remain an important part of Mexican literary history.

Hayden Herrera, suspects Kahlo may have once again taken "poetic license"), the sounds of hissing bullets and the sights of bloody soldiers were part of her childhood experience. So were *corridos*, or revolutionary ballads, Kahlo would sing in support of the Zapatista cause. By Kahlo's account, she grew up amidst a sense of Mexican revolutionary spirit.

Nevertheless, it was the overthrown Díaz government that had given Kahlo's father the opportunity to earn a living as a photographer. The work Guillermo Kahlo received from the administration paid well. But after 1911, jobs were hard to come by. The family had to take out a loan against their house, sell furniture, and even take in guests to generate a little extra income.

PREP SCHOOL FRIDA

For a girl whose name meant "peace," Kahlo's early life embodied much turmoil. In her journal, she recalled an embarrassing situation that occurred after a kindergarten astronomy lesson involving the sun, the earth, and the moon. "It made such an impression on me that I urinated," Kahlo said of the lecture. "They took off my wet pants and put on the pants of a girl who lived across the street from my house. Because of this, I took such a dislike to the girl that one day I brought her near my house and I began to strangle her. Her tongue was already out of her mouth when a baker passed by and freed her from my hands."

At age six, Frida contracted polio, leaving her bedridden for nine months. However, her doting father made her swim and ride a bicycle—sometimes to the point of exhaustion—to strengthen her limbs.

Before her disease, Frida was what one *Smithsonian* magazine contributor described as "a chubby child with a winning smile and sparkling eyes." But polio made her thin, and her leg withered. When she entered a German elementary school, the children gave her a humiliating nickname: Pata de Palo

(Wooden Leg). It's not surprising that Frida felt lonely and isolated. During this period, she created an imaginary play-mate. She would blow on a windowpane and draw a door on the foggy glass. She imagined herself going through the door and running across a plain to a building, which she entered to find her friend.

"I no longer remember her form and coloring, but I do know that she was a lot of fun and laughed a great deal, sound-lessly, of course," she wrote years later. "She was very nimble and could dance."

Frida's life changed dramatically when her father decided to send her to the Escuela Nacional Preparatoria (National Preparatory School), an excellent preparatory school in Mexico City attended by the most privileged of the city's young. Her mother opposed the move because there were some 300 boys in the school and only a handful of girls. But Frida easily passed the entrance examination and entered an institution where her intellectual curiosity and interest in the arts would be satisfied. She decided that she eventually wanted to study medicine.

Frida was a rebellious teenager, setting her own style of dress, sometimes designing her own clothes, and often appear-ing in men's suits, her long black hair pulled back in a severe bun. She was attractive in an unusual way. Her dark eyebrows met in the middle, and she didn't bother to pluck them. She also had a faint mustache that she did not hesitate to include in her many self-portraits.

She defied convention from the start and was fortunate to fall in with a band of intellectual and mischievous class-mates at school who were also defying convention. They called themselves the Cachuchas, named after the jaunty caps they wore. This group, comprised of seven boys and two girls, were both the pride and despair of the Preparatoria: pride because of their academic accomplishments, despair because of the mischief they liked to get into. In one of their pranks, they

The penetrating eyes of the school-aged Kahlo denote the sharp mind of the woman she was to become. Kahlo was one of only two young women in the Cachuchas, the rebellious prep school circle whose members devoted themselves to the cerebral pursuits of literature and socialist-nationalist ideas.

tied firecrackers to the tail of a dog, lit them, and sent the poor animal running through the corridors.

On another occasion, they decided to teach a lesson to a professor whom they considered boring. They detonated a firecracker above the podium where he was lecturing. The blast knocked out windows above the lectern, and glass showered the professor. However, he merely smoothed down his mussed hair, brushed the glass from his clothing, and went on with his boring lecture.

The Cachuchas disdained politics as beneath them, but they espoused a kind of romantic socialism combined with nationalism. They were influenced by the ideals of the revolution and considered themselves disciples of José Vasconcelos, minister of public education under President Alvaro Obregón. Vasconcelos's aim was to make Mexican education truly Mexican, turning away from European influences. The Cachuchas heartily agreed with this philosophy. In addition to being rebels and mischief-makers, members of the Cachuchas reveled in being intellectually curious.

Being accepted by the Cachuchas was a great honor for Frida Kahlo. The members would make names for themselves as adults, becoming professionals, educators, leaders of the nation, artists, and writers. They obviously liked Frida's intellectual curiosity, as well as her rebellious nature.

The leader of the group was Alejandro Gómez Arias, who was to be her first great love and the friend who was with her on the fateful day of the streetcar accident. Gómez Arias would go on to become a highly regarded intellectual, lawyer, and political journalist.

Frida also enjoyed the company of other groups at the school. Among them was the Contemporáneos, an informal literary club, many of whose members would go on to make their mark in Mexican literature, politics, and the arts. Another group was the Maistros, a more radical band of free thinkers.

Still, her real pals were the Cachuchas, whose favorite hangout was the Ibero American Library, a short distance from the school. There they would argue, flirt, write papers, draw pictures and, most of all, read. They read everything. They devoured the works of many of the most famous authors of the world: Germans, Russians, French, English, Americans, and, of course, Mexicans. Frida learned to read in three languages—Spanish, English, and German. Remembering her father's collection of philosophical treatises, she loved to discuss Hegel and Kant, among other great thinkers. She would call out the school window to Gómez Arias, "Alejandro, lend me your Spengler. I don't have anything to read on the bus." That no doubt would have been Oswald Spengler's *Decline of the West*, written by the German philosopher in 1918. Regrettably, the book was greatly admired by the Nazis.

The Cachuchas had competitions among themselves and their friends to find the best book and see who could read it first. They held dramatizations of what they read, attracting a wide and admiring audience.

One of Frida's few female friends was the other girl in the Cachuchas, Carmen Jaime, a very eccentric but interesting young lady who would grow up to become a scholar of seventeenth-century Spanish literature. She dressed in dark, masculine clothing and earned the nicknames "James" because of her manly attire and "Vampire" because she sometimes wore a black cape. Carmen was just the kind of person Frida, herself an eccentric, would find interesting. Carmen seemed to have read every philosophy book ever written, and their discussions would leave lesser minds in the dust.

Frida was able to earn high marks in school without putting in much effort. She had the enviable ability to read a text and easily remember its contents. She was presumptuous enough on occasion to urge the school's director to remove professors she found boring and ill informed. Needless to say, such behavior did not endear her to many of the teachers.

In 1922, Frida had her first reported encounter with Diego Rivera, who, along with several other artists, had been hired by Vasconcelos to paint a mural in the school's Bolivar Amphitheater that reflected Mexican culture. Kahlo claimed she became infatuated with Rivera around that time, going so far as having wished to one day bear him a child. At the time, such a pairing may have seemed unlikely. Kahlo was a teen, and Rivera was 36 years old.

Diego Rivera, Kahlo's Destiny

Diego Rivera might have been world famous when he began to paint a mural in Frida's National Preparatory School, the Prepartoria, but he didn't look the part. At 36, he was enormously fat, and he dressed like a slob. In those days, teachers and officials of the school were always properly dressed, the men often in homburg hats (felt hats with stiff, curled brims), black suits, and stiff collars. Rivera favored a floppy Stetson (broad-brimmed felt hat), baggy pants held up by a wide leather belt—sometimes a cartridge belt—and heavy black miner's boots. His wrinkled clothes looked as if he'd slept in them for a week. How could he help but be the subject of student fun at the hands of the mischievous Cachuchas and their most irreverent member, Frida Kahlo?

Rivera's Preparatoria mural was his first, the product of liberal minister of public education José Vasconcelos's desire to commission murals as part of an overarching strategy to bring truly Mexican art to the country. Rivera called his debut mural *Creation*. It was a 1,000-square-foot (92.9-sq.-meter) work of art that was strongly influenced by European, especially Italian, styles, with a blend of early Mexican art. Rivera's model for Eve was his mistress, Lupe Marín, soon to be his wife. He painted her in the nude.

KAHLO'S TRICKS

Unfortunately for Rivera, he and other artists who painted at the Preparatoria were like sitting ducks for student pranksters. High up on their scaffolds, they were at the mercy of whatever mischief was going on below them, despite the fact that students were banned from the amphitheater while the work was in progress. Sometimes the pranks caused serious damage. For instance, after a scaffold was built, wood chips and shavings were often left scattered about the floor. The students would set these on fire, and sometimes a fire would badly damage the scaffolding and the work in progress. Some of the artists began carrying guns.

Because of his appearance and his habit of talking while working, Diego Rivera became an especially choice object of student shenanigans, especially for Frida Kahlo, who took a particular pleasure in targeting him. Once she soaped the stairway that led to the amphitheater stage, where he was working on *Creation*. But Rivera, being the fat man that he was, was always careful where he walked and didn't slip on the soap. However, the same professor who was the subject of the student firecracker trick because of his boring lectures slipped on the soap and fell down the stairs.

Kahlo was intrigued by the beautiful models who accompanied Rivera on the scaffold to pose for him. Besides Lupe Marín, there was Nahui Olin, a well-known Mexican beauty. Kahlo delighted in using the presence of these models to tease Rivera. If Marín was on the scaffold, Kahlo would shout to him, "Hey, Diego, here comes Nahui!" If Diego was alone on

Diego Rivera, already a famous painter, captured the attention of 15-year-old Kahlo when he was commissioned to paint a mural at the school where Kahlo was a student. Rather than being repulsed by Rivera's slovenly dress and round belly, Kahlo found the robust artist fascinating.

the scaffold and she saw Marín arriving, she would call out, "Watch out, Diego, Lupe's coming!" as if he was up to no good and was about to be caught.

Kahlo obviously found Rivera fascinating, as did many women over the years. She once reportedly told a group of fellow students that her ambition was to have Rivera's baby. The other students, especially the girls, were appalled. How could she be attracted to such a slovenly man, years older than her? Their reactions didn't bother Kahlo. "Diego is so gentle, so tender, so wise, so sweet," she said. "I'd bathe him and clean him."

Later, Kahlo remembered that even while she taunted him and called him names, she was thinking to herself, "You'll see, *panzon* (fat belly), now you don't pay any attention to me, but one day I'll have a child by you." One of Kahlo's great tragedies, of course, was that, because of her accident, she couldn't have a child by anyone.

RIVERA TAKES NOTICE OF YOUNG KAHLO

Rivera recalled being amused by the impish little girl who came to visit him while he was working. In his autobiography, *My Art, My Life,* he recalled seeing Kahlo one day burst through the auditorium door and come striding up to where he was working and where Marín was quietly knitting.

"She was dressed like any other high school student, but her manner immediately set her apart," he wrote. "She had unusual dignity and self-assurance, and there was a strange fire in her eyes." She asked permission to watch him work, and he said he would be charmed. Marín, however, began to be jealous and started to insult the girl. Kahlo paid no attention, and Marín herself was intrigued. "Look at that girl! Small as she is, she does not fear a tall, strong woman like me," Rivera quoted her as saying. "I like her."

Kahlo first encountered Rivera in 1922. At that time, Rivera was a well-known artist whose work was in galleries and private hands around the world. He had studied in Spain and Paris, where he became friends with such renowned artists as Pablo Picasso and Amadeo Modigliani. His years abroad saw many dramatic upheavals in the world—World War I, which changed Europe forever, and the Russian Revolution, led by Vladimir Ilych Lenin and Leon Trotsky, who would one day go to Mexico and have a profound impact on both Rivera and Kahlo. In Rivera's native Mexico, he saw long years of violent change in both government and society after the Revolution of 1910.

YOUNG RIVERA

Diego Rivera was born on December 8, 1886, in Guanajuato, an old mining city in the Sierra Madres, 170 miles (273 km) northwest of Mexico City. He was fortunate to have a father, also named Diego, who encouraged his early interest in art. He studied art at the Academy of San Carlos and began to sell his paintings while still a teenager.

In 1906, his father showed some of his work to the governor of Veracruz, Teodoro Dehesa, who was greatly impressed. Dehesa offered to give the young artist a monthly allowance to study in Europe. Rivera, then 20, earned money for the passage to Spain by selling his work at two exhibits. It was thus that his European experience began. While in Europe, Rivera had many romances. People were attracted to this robust, outgoing, intelligent, and well-read "cowboy" from Mexico. In Paris, he lived with a Russian artist named Angeline Beloff, who bore him a son, Diego Jr., who died before he reached two years of age. But the artist also met and wooed several other women. Kahlo was not to be even among his first.

In 1910, Rivera returned to Mexico for the centennial celebration of Mexico's independence from Spain. He would show his work at his old school, the Academy of San Carlos. The day the exhibit opened, November 20, 1910, Francisco Madero called for a general uprising against the dictatorial rule of Porfirio Díaz—the beginning of the Mexican Revolution, today, a national holiday.

Revolutionary forces were winning battles against Díaz's army. In the north, Francisco "Pancho" Villa and Alvaro Obregón, future president of Mexico, were the revolutionary heroes, while in the south, Emiliano Zapata commanded a large following.

In honor of the revolution, Rivera designed a poster showing a family plowing a field while an image of Jesus looked down on them. The poster read, "The Distribution of Land to the Poor Is Not Contrary to the Teachings of Our Lord Jesus Christ and the Holy Mother Church." It was mass-produced and widely distributed. Rivera also visited Zapata in the state of Morelos and was impressed by the communes that the legendary leader had set up to work the land. Working together without bosses, the farmers produced sugar on a large scale for eight years. Rivera painted a portrait of Zapata, who was killed in an ambush on April 10, 1919.

An allowance Rivera had been receiving from the government of Francisco Madero was cut off when Madero was assassinated in 1913. And just two months after Rivera's one-man show in Paris, Archduke Francis Ferdinand of Austria was shot and killed, an event that would lead to World War I.

After a brief sojourn on the island of Majorca, Rivera and Angeline Beloff returned to Paris to find a nation at war. Times were tough for everyone, and Rivera and Beloff had

CUBISM

Rivera experimented with cubism, an art form in which figures are depicted as fragmented objects in space. Pablo Picasso and Georges Braque were behind the cubist movement. Rivera plunged into it with his usual ferocious energy and produced about 200 cubist paintings. He became an important part of the cubist movement. Working at a fast pace, he would produce as many as five paintings a month in this style. Through Picasso's influence, he was given a one-man show at Paris's Galerie Weill in April 1914. Despite his success with cubism, Rivera gradually became disillusioned with this art form when he realized, as he put it, "all this innovation had little to do with real life." He decided that the work of Picasso and the other cubists was for the wealthy. Rivera wanted to paint for the people.

Confined to bed following her accident, Kahlo painted using an easel and a mirror her mother rigged overhead. Thus began Kahlo's focus on painting self-portraits, such as this one from 1929.

trouble making ends meet. Millions of men and women were being slaughtered in that brutal war, and nobody was in the mood to buy art. Rivera met the French artist Henri Matisse and the revolutionary Russian writer Ilya Ehrenburg. He had a fling with a Russian artist, Marvena Vorobev-Stebelska, but, after living with her for a short time, returned to Beloff. Such behavior was typical of the way Rivera dealt with women through most of his life, finding stable relationships but always veering off to play with a more exciting lady, then returning to stability.

Events were multiplying in Europe. French soldiers, sick of war, staged a mutiny. The United States declared war on Germany. And, in Russia, Leon Trotsky led thousands of workers in a successful insurrection, taking over Moscow. It was October 25, 1917, the start of the Russian Revolution, which would have such a profound effect on the entire world.

Rivera and his Russian friends were excited. Lenin promised to give the peasants land and put the workers in charge of industry. That was the Communist ideal. On March 3, 1918, Trotsky signed a separate peace with Germany. But World War I ended eight months later, on November 11, 1918, when Germany agreed to an armistice with all of its enemies.

While still living in Paris, Rivera met the muralist David Alfaro Siqueiros, who also went to the Academy of San Carlos. Siqueiros was now 21, and he and Rivera became close friends. Siqueiros had fought with the armies of Alvaro Obregón and had attained the rank of captain. He regaled Rivera with stories of the Mexican Revolution, in which 2 million people had died.

RETURN TO MEXICO

Rivera began to realize that he had to return to Mexico. Obregón was elected president in 1920, and Rivera believed the time was ripe for a new era of Mexican art. After a 17-month tour of Italy studying Renaissance art, he left Angeline Beloff in June and returned to his native land. He came to realize how badly he had treated Beloff. "She gave me everything a good woman can give to a man," he later wrote. "In return, she received from me all the heartache and misery that a man can inflict upon a woman." Beloff lived alone for the rest of her life. Rivera never returned to her.

When he arrived in Mexico, Rivera was greeted by José Vasconcelos, Obregón's minister of public education, who asked him to do a mural at the National Preparatory School, where the mischievous young Frida Kahlo was a star student.

4

Sundays with the "Little Devil"

Alejandro Gómez Arias was the "big man on campus" at the Preparatoria. Handsome and smart, he was the center of attention among the cliques of bright young students who were destined to find important roles for themselves as adults. He was adept at conversation, whether discussing literature, philosophy, art, or just school gossip. Fellow students tended to hang on his every word. Gómez Arias was also very nationalistic. He urged his friends to dedicate themselves to the "great destiny" of Mexico. Kahlo was attracted to him, as she was always attracted to the star of the show, to the great and near-great, who always seemed to cluster about her. Gómez Arias remembered her as having a "childlike manner, but at the same time she was quick and dramatic in her urge to discover life."

He was several classes ahead of Kahlo, which seemed to add to his attractiveness. She always gravitated toward older, more experienced, and worldly men. Not that Gómez Arias was a man in those days, but he was obviously on his way to being an important one someday. Kahlo wrote many letters to him, many of which were accompanied by drawings. "You can see what progress I am making in drawing," she wrote. "Now you know that I am a prodigy in matters of art." It was during the summer of 1923 that their relationship deepened into love. She began to refer to Gómez Arias as her fiancé.

On November 30, 1923, there was a rebellion against President Obregón that brought fighting to Mexico City. Vasconcelos resigned during the fighting but returned to his job briefly after the insurrection was put down (with 7,000 dead). But he quit again when Plutarco Elías Calles became president. To protest his resignation, students at the Preparatoria took out their anger on the murals in the school, scratching curses into the plaster and spitting on them. Kahlo didn't take part in any of these demonstrations. Her parents kept her at home.

Kahlo's letters to Gómez Arias were full of love and yearning, as if she had a premonition that their relationship was doomed. Her passionate letters to him continued while she was recovering from the streetcar accident on September 17, 1925, which put her in the hospital for a month and then kept her confined to her home in Coyoacán.

On December 18, three months after the accident, Kahlo was well enough to visit Mexico City. Since she had missed her final examinations at the Preparatoria, she did not go back to the school. Her family needed money and she went to work. She helped her father in his photographic studio and took other part-time jobs. Kahlo and Gómez Arias were drifting further apart. He apparently accused her of having affairs with other men, which she admitted.

"Although I have said, 'I love you' to many, and I have had dates with and kissed others, underneath it all I never loved anyone but you," she wrote to Gómez Arias in December 1925.

It was while trying to bring Gómez Arias back to her that she painted her first self-portrait. She started it in the summer

Kahlo's first love, Alejandro Gómez Arias, speaks to the Congreso de Mérida. Gómez Arias stole Kahlo's heart with his magnetic personality and the passionate rhetoric that would later benefit his political life. It was for Gómez Arias that Kahlo painted her first self-portrait, a gift she hoped would persuade him to return to her, despite her infidelities.

of 1926, when she became ill and had to be confined to her home. She finished it the next September.

KAHLO'S RECOVERY

From the time of her accident, Kahlo was in almost constant pain, and she had numerous relapses that put her back in the hospital. She began her self-portrait after doctors found that three of her vertebrae were out of place and she had to be placed in casts again. She turned to painting as a way to overcome her boredom and loneliness. She used oil paints and brushes that her father, an amateur artist, kept in his studio. Her first subjects—besides herself—were friends she had known in school.

In letters to Gómez Arias in this period, she describes her pain: "I'm fed up with so much sickness, like an old woman, I don't know how I'll be when I'm 30, you'll have to carry me all day wrapped in cotton. . . ." But Gómez Arias left for Germany and was gone for several months. There is some speculation that his parents sent him to Europe to cool off his relationship with Kahlo, of whom they didn't approve. Her letters to him continued to describe her loneliness and pain, and she begged him to love her. But Kahlo and Gómez Arias drifted further and further apart. Gómez Arias was kept busy with his university studies, and Kahlo with her art.

A year after Kahlo's accident she asked Gómez Arias why he was studying so much. She wondered what he expected to learn about life. She described her own lost hope of finding anything behind the emptiness of daily experience:

A little while ago, not much more than a few days ago, I was a child who went about in a world of colors, of hard and tangible

FIRST SELF-PORTRAIT

Unlike many of her later self-portraits, Frida Kahlo's first self-portrait finds her in a more formal pose. She has made herself look elegant, garbed in a wine-red velvet dress with an elegant brocade collar and looking quite beautiful. Like several of her later self-portraits, it was a gift to a man whom she was begging to love her—in the painting, she depicts herself holding out her right hand as a sort of offering. On the back of the piece she wrote, "Frieda Kahlo at 17 years of age in September 1926. Coyoacán." Beneath it were the German words *Heute ist Immer Noch* (Today Still Goes On).

Kahlo was actually 19, her falsehood stemming from her lifelong habit of subtracting two or three years from her age so she seemed to have been born in 1910, at the outbreak of the Mexican Revolution, not her real birth year of 1907.

forms. Everything was mysterious and something was hidden. Guessing what it was was a game for me.

If you knew how terrible it is to know suddenly, as if a bolt of lightning elucidated the earth. Now I live in a painful planet, transparent as ice, but it is as if I had learned everything at once in seconds. My friends, my companions became women slowly, I became old in instants and everything today is bland and lucid. I know that nothing lies behind. If there was something, I would see it. . . .

Even so, Kahlo's inner spirit refused to give in. Despite her pain, she was an inspiration to her friends. One of them, Aurora Reyes, remembered that Kahlo "always acted happy, she gave her heart. She had an incredible richness, and though one went to see her to console her, one came away consoled." Another friend, Adelina Reyes, said, "When we went to visit her when she was sick, she played, she laughed, she commented, she made caustic criticisms, witticisms, and wise opinions. If she cried, no one knew it."

KAHLO REENTERS LIFE

Late in 1927, Kahlo had recuperated enough to resume something of a normal life. At that time, many of her old friends from the Preparatoria, including Gómez Arias, were involved in Mexican politics, which frequently turned violent. Kahlo became friendly with a young student demonstrator named German de Campo. He was a fiery speaker who was always elegantly dressed, usually with a flower in his buttonhole, and sporting a cane. It was de Campo who introduced Kahlo to his friend, Tina Modotti. Modotti was an Italian-born American photographer, very beautiful and very independent. She had come to Mexico with her lover, a famous photographer named Edward Weston. When Weston returned to the United States, she stayed on in Mexico.

Frida Kahlo soon became involved with the artists, writers, and political activists who had gathered around the revolutionary Cuban Communist Julio Antonio Mella. Mella and Alejandro Gómez Arias were law students together. They were both opposed to the government of Plutarco Elías Calles, president of Mexico from 1924 to 1928. But Gómez Arias didn't approve of many of the radicals in this group and was not really a part of it. This was another factor that led to the eventual end of his relationship with Kahlo. Unlike her former boyfriend, Kahlo was strongly attracted to these people—and to the Communist Party.

REACQUAINTANCE WITH DIEGO RIVERA

As it has been said, death and violence were part of the life of Mexico in those days. German de Campo was murdered by agents of Calles for his antigovernment speeches. And on January 10, 1929, Mella was shot down by a Cuban gunman while walking on a Mexico City street with Modotti.

In the time leading up to that murder, Kahlo and Modotti became good friends. Kahlo admired the older woman's spirit and energy. She began to attend parties and meetings of the artists and political activists, many of whom were either Communists or had strong Communist leanings. Among the artists who attended these get-togethers were the muralists José Clemente Orozco, David Alfaro Siqueiros and, of course, Diego Rivera. It's generally believed that Kahlo became reacquainted with Rivera at these parties. Rivera had joined the Communist Party in 1922, and he had contributed artwork to the cause. He also gave rousing speeches to workers. Some called him the "Lenin of Mexico."

Though the imaginative Kahlo and Rivera each told their own stories regarding the circumstances that led to their romance, biographer Hayden Herrera suggests this likely took place at one of Modotti's parties. According to an account of Kahlo's relayed in a 1954 Mexican newspaper article, Rivera caught her attention at one of the gatherings by shooting a phonograph with a pistol. Everybody was carrying pistols in those days, Kahlo explained. They'd shoot out street lamps or

After her recovery, Kahlo became deeply involved with the Communist Party. It was through her involvement with the party that she became reacquainted with Diego Rivera, from whom she sought advice regarding her potential as an artist.

take potshots at signs and anything else in the streets that made itself a likely target.

In another of Kahlo's recollections, she said she had once taken several paintings to Rivera while he was working on a mural at the Ministry of Public Education. She was hoping to get his expert opinion.

"Without more ado I said: 'Diego, come down,'" she wrote, "And just the way he is, so humble, so amiable, he came down. 'Look, I have not come to flirt or anything even if you are a woman-chaser. I have come to show you my painting. If you are interested in it, tell me so, if not, likewise, so that I will go to work at something else to help my parents.'"

In his autobiography *My Art, My Life*, Rivera relayed a similar anecdote, explaining how he was impressed with the three portraits Kahlo had shown him. But of these, according to Kahlo, Rivera liked the self-portrait best. The others, he told her, were too much influenced by other artists. He asked her to paint another picture and he would come to her home on Sunday.

Thus began a legendary relationship between two great Mexican artists; Rivera's subsequent visit to the Casa Azul in Coyoacán was the beginning of a courtship. From then on, he came every Sunday for a visit.

One day, Kahlo's father, Guillermo, took Rivera aside and said, "I've got the feeling that you're interested in my daughter, is that so?"

"I certainly am," Rivera replied, "otherwise I wouldn't come all the way to Coyoacán so often."

"Do you realize she's a little devil?" Guillermo asked him.

"I know," Rivera said.

"All right, you've been warned," Guillermo said.

It's not known exactly when it dawned on Rivera that this young lady (she was 21; he was 41) was the impish little girl who had tormented him back in 1922 when he was painting at her school.

Kahlo once said she suffered two serious accidents in her life. One was the streetcar crash that crippled her for life and the second was meeting Diego Rivera. Her life with this strong man and her determination to emerge from his shadow and earn recognition for her artistic talent were about to begin.

5

The Elephant and the Dove

Frida Kahlo and Diego Rivera were married on August 21,
1929, in Kahlo's hometown of Coyoacán. The wedding was a
civil ceremony, the only kind recognized in Mexico after the
revolution. Kahlo and Rivera had fallen in love rather quickly
after Rivera had begun visiting her to talk about her painting.
Rivera was later to say that Kahlo became "the most important
thing in my life." Unfortunately, he didn't always show it by
his behavior.

By this time, Rivera had had many relationships with
women, including a church marriage to Lupe Marín, which
wasn't considered legal. He had a son by his Russian mistress,
Angeline Beloff, and a daughter by the Russian artist Marevna
Vorobev-Stebelska. His son died before reaching age two,
and Rivera didn't acknowledge his daughter as being his own
for many years. These incidents were only the beginning of
Rivera's messy relationships with the opposite sex. He seemed

to sincerely love Kahlo, however, and despite having many affairs with other women during their marriage, he loved her until her death.

Kahlo's religious mother refused to attend the ceremony in the Coyoacán town hall because it was a civil ceremony, but her father was there. Guillermo Kahlo gave Rivera another piece of advice before the ceremony began.

"Now, look, my daughter is a sick person and all her life she's going to be sick," he said. "She's intelligent but not pretty. Think it over if you like, and if you still wish to marry her, marry her, I give you my permission."

Kahlo, whose style of dress changed frequently over the years, depending on her mood and her political views, had to borrow clothes for the wedding. She borrowed a skirt, blouse, and *rebozo,* a Mexican stole, from her maid. In a photo accompanying a wedding announcement in the Mexico City newspaper *Le Prensa,* she holds a cigarette. The wedding day turned out to be a poor start to a marriage. First of all, Rivera's former wife, Lupe Marín, showed up and made a scene. She compared her physical attributes with Kahlo's, describing her own as more attractive, and stormed out. Then Rivera proceeded to get very drunk at the wedding party at the home of Roberto Montenegro. He fired his pistol, scaring the guests, broke a man's finger, and destroyed some furnishings. Kahlo and Rivera got into a fight, and she ran away in tears. They didn't get together again for several days.

Despite the shaky start, their marriage made the society columns of newspapers around the world. Diego Rivera was famous, even though his wife was not well known at the time. When photographer Tina Modotti wrote to Edward Weston in September 1929 to tell him about the wedding, she didn't even mention Frida Kahlo by name, but just referred to her as a "lovely nineteen-year-old girl, of German father and Mexican mother, a painter herself." Then she added in Spanish, "A ver que sale" (Let's see how it works).

Kahlo's friends were shocked that she would take as her husband this fat, homely, *old* man. They considered the union *una cosa monstruosa* (a hideous thing). Many said the union was like a marriage between an elephant and a dove. But for Kahlo's parents, ill and in bad financial straits, things worked out quite well. Rivera went on to pay off their mortgage and help them in other ways. As for Kahlo, marriage to the famous artist meant she could travel in Mexican, American, and European artistic and intellectual circles. She enjoyed the attention she received as the wife of Diego Rivera, although she would soon be eager to be recognized as an artist in her own right.

CHANGING STYLE OF DRESS AND ART

It's interesting to notice how Kahlo's manner of dress reflected the changing conditions of her life. In her teenage years, she had sometimes worn men's clothing. After her first introduction to the Communist Party, a political party that does not believe in private ownership, she took to wearing the plain red shirt of the party, with her hair cut short and pulled tightly back. In fact, a painting by Rivera, *Ballad of the Revolution*, in 1928 shows her in this severe costume, the red star of Communism on her shirt, passing out guns to workers.

But after their marriage, Rivera encouraged Kahlo to adopt the colorful Mexican-Indian costumes worn by the women of the Isthmus of Tehuantepec. For most of the rest of her life, Kahlo dressed in the Tehuana Indian manner, with flowing skirts and dramatic jewelry of silver and jade. She wore her hair swept up and decorated with ribbons, flowers, and combs. She frequently painted self-portraits of herself in those exotic costumes, and she certainly attracted attention on the streets, not only of Mexico City, but of cities in the United States and Europe. One observer said she made herself into a work of art.

Rivera, on the other hand, dressed in attire that was much more subdued. For most of his life he dressed in clothes that

Kahlo and Rivera pose in 1931, shortly after their marriage. Though few of Kahlo's friends could understand her attraction to the large, homely Rivera, it was Kahlo's adolescent wish to be Rivera's wife. The union also proved beneficial for Kahlo's family, whom Rivera assisted financially.

"made him look like a western sheriff or rancher," as writer
Jack Rummel aptly described. Otherwise, he wore cheap business suits that made him look "like a receiving clerk at a Ford
Factory, not in the least bit influenced by 'authentic' Indian
dress."

Some critics have argued that Rivera was an influence on
Kahlo's early art. They point to Kahlo's painting entitled *The
Bus,* an almost mural-like painting done in 1929 of people
sitting in a row on a bus. Not only is Rivera's muralistic style
there, but also his political views. A well-dressed man holding
a bag of coins represents capitalism. Seated next to him is a
pretty woman who might be his "trophy" wife or his girlfriend.
The other figures include a barefoot peasant woman, a worker
holding a wrench, a housewife with a market basket, and a boy
looking out of the window. Unlike Rivera's sweeping wall-
sized murals, however, *The Bus* is only 10 ¼ by 22 inches.

Among Kahlo's other notable paintings of this period
was *Portrait of Virginia (Nina),* depicting a lovely little girl
who, interestingly enough, has Kahlo's famous eyebrows. An
unusual touch is that her dress is held together by a safety
pin. Another work of that period is an amazing portrait of the
agriculturist Luther Burbank. It shows him as half-man, half-
vegetable, rising out of his own corpse. This painting, done in
1931, is considered by critics to represent a turning point in
Kahlo's art career. From then on, she would follow her own
vision of reality.

It has to be said, too, that Rivera encouraged his wife
to go her own way in art, not to copy him or any other artist. And there was never any hint that he was jealous of her
accomplishments.

SETTING UP THEIR HOME

After the wild wedding day and a brief, angry separation, the
couple moved into Rivera's house on the first block of Paseo
de la Reforma in Mexico City. "For furniture, we had a narrow
bed, a dining set that Frances Toor gave us, with a long black

table, and a little yellow kitchen table that my mother gave us," Kahlo said in an interview. (Toor was editor of *Mexican Folkways* magazine.) She said the table was used for Rivera's extensive collection of archaeological specimens. He was an avid collector of pieces of Mexican history he encountered on his travels around the country. Kahlo and Rivera weren't the only ones staying at the home. According to Kahlo, there was also a live-in maid and, for some time, the painter David Alfaro Siqueiros, his wife, and two other Communists.

Kahlo was a devoted wife, and she was upset when she discovered she wasn't able to have Rivera's baby. She had an abortion after three months of pregnancy when it was learned the fetus was in the wrong position.

LUTHER BURBANK

Until she painted the American horticulturist Luther Burbank, Kahlo had painted only people she knew. But her choice of the plant scientist as a subject is not surprising. According to an article published in 2001 by the art scholar Lucretia Hoover Giese, Burbank had made a career of developing new varieties of vegetables and fruits by grafting or cross-breeding two existing ones. It seems natural that Kahlo, who came from mixed European and Mexican heritage, would be interested in the agriculturist's work.

Interestingly, Rivera also featured Burbank in a mural that he had completed around the same time as Kahlo's painting. That work, *Allegory of California*, made its debut at the Pacific Stock Exchange Lunch Club in February 1931. It depicted Burbank as one of several scientists, lumberjacks, miners, and others utilizing the state's natural resources. Giese pointed out a significant difference in Rivera's and Kahlo's treatment of their subject. Where Rivera shows Burbank as a "doer," kneeling over a plant he is working with, Kahlo portrays him as an embodiment of his pursuits.

"I cried inconsolably," she said. "But I distracted myself fixing meals, cleaning house, painting at times, and going along with Diego each day to the scaffolds."

By this time, Rivera was working on a commission to decorate the stairwell at the National Palace in Mexico City with murals. It was to be a narrative history of Mexico, and he was to work on these murals into the 1940s. They illustrate in dramatic figures and blazing colors the country's history from before the Spanish conquest into the turmoil of the 1920s and 1930s. The way he shows the struggle of the Mexican people against their oppressors strongly reflects his Communist leanings, but no one seemed to mind. Much later in New York City, someone did mind, and the fight between Rivera and Nelson Rockefeller would become the stuff of legend.

Meanwhile, Kahlo was playing the dutiful housewife. She visited her husband on the scaffolds, taking him his lunch and commenting on his work. "He really liked me to come along bringing his lunch in a basket covered with flowers," she said. Rivera's former wife, Lupe Marín, had put that idea into Kahlo's head. After the scene at the wedding, Marín became Kahlo's good friend and even helped her furnish their house.

Rivera also enjoyed having his wife comment on his painting and often took her criticism to heart.

KAHLO SPARKLES

One of the key figures in Rivera's mural was Emiliano Zapata, the Mexican revolutionary from the state of Morelos. The artist depicted Zapata as leading a white horse. In actuality, Zapata's horse was black, and Kahlo pointed out this discrepancy. "Diego, how can you paint Zapata's horse white?" she demanded. He gave her a lame excuse, basically that he thought it looked better white, and the horse remained that color. However, when she complained that the horse's legs were too thick, he handed over his paintbrush and let her repaint the animal's legs.

Kahlo's personality at that time was described by her friend Luis Cardoza y Aragón: "Frida was what she always was, a marvelous woman. There was a spark in her that was growing and beginning to light up her canvases, to light up her life and, in turn, the lives of others." It's interesting that so many of her friends described how they felt better by simply being in her presence.

RIVERA'S POLITICAL AND DOMESTIC TROUBLES

Rivera got in trouble with his Communist comrades for accepting commissions from the Mexican government, associating with capitalists, and accepting their money. This was to be a lifelong conflict between Rivera's opposition to capitalism and his eagerness to take capitalists' money so he could paint the murals that he felt needed to be painted.

He was finally kicked out of the party. But in typical Rivera fashion, he turned his expulsion into theater. He went to a party convention in 1929 armed with what looked like a pistol concealed under a handkerchief. By this time, he held a high position in the party. He sat down and launched into a speech:

> I, Diego Rivera, general secretary of the Communist Party of Mexico, accuse the painter Diego Rivera of collaboration with the petty bourgeois Mexican government. He accepted a commission to decorate the stairwell of the National Palace. This contravenes the interests of the Comintern. Therefore, the painter Diego Rivera must be expelled from the Communist Party by the general secretary, Diego Rivera.

He then stood up and exposed the "pistol." He smashed it into pieces and walked out. The pistol was made of clay. (*Bourgeois* is French for the "middle class," but it carries a negative meaning. *Comintern* refers to the first congress of the Communist Party in 1919, formed to take control of the Communist movement throughout the world. *Contravene* means to act in opposition to something.)

Despite his flippant behavior, Rivera was deeply hurt by his expulsion from the Communist Party because he felt he remained loyal to its principles. Kahlo, who had joined the party in 1928, quit in solidarity with her husband.

While Kahlo was suffering through her abortion, she learned that Rivera was having an affair with one of his assistants. These were two serious blows to her—one, that she probably could never have a child, and two, that she could never trust Rivera to be faithful to her. Kahlo was either going to have to live with his infidelities or get away from him entirely. She would always be torn by these two unsatisfactory choices.

In the fall of 1930, she and Rivera left Mexico for their first visit to the United States. It would be another important milestone in Kahlo's life, with experiences both high and low.

COMING TO THE UNITED STATES

When Frida Kahlo and Diego Rivera arrived in San Francisco in November 1930, they found a country in the throes of the Great Depression. The stock market had crashed in October 1929 and sent the economy reeling. Unemployment was above 20 percent, and there were bread and soup lines in San Francisco when the Riveras arrived.

The couple was not directly affected by the crumpled economy. Rivera had commissions to paint murals in the San Francisco Stock Exchange and the California School of Fine Arts, which later became the San Francisco Art Institute. Although he liked to say he arrived in the United States as a "spy" to spread his revolutionary ideas, Rivera actually was fascinated by the achievements of capitalism, particularly heavy industry and the machinery that made it run. He loved to include in his paintings massive machines and the strong men who worked them. Rivera once said, "Perhaps future generations will recognize the machine as the art of our day."

The rich business people who hired Rivera didn't seem to mind that he was a devoted Communist, the "Lenin of

Rivera was commissioned to paint the stairwells of Mexico City's National Palace with patriotic murals. His success spread to the United States, where he was commissioned to paint several large-scale works. In this photo, Rivera paints a mural depicting California's contributions to the nation.

Mexico." They didn't seem to care that he showed images of the great industrialists, John D. Rockefeller Jr., Henry Ford, and J.P. Morgan, as grotesque caricatures in his paintings or that he filled his murals with the hammer-and-sickle symbol of Communism and pictures of Communist leaders. It wasn't until his run-in with John D. Rockefeller Jr.'s son, Nelson Rockefeller, that Rivera's ideas were seriously challenged.

Actually, Rivera's behavior at this time angered the Communists more than it did the capitalists. He was criticized as being the "painter for millionaires" and for consorting with the Mexican government, now controlled by the reactionary Calles administration.

In Mexico, Communists, their sympathizers, and even union supporters were frequently arrested, deported, or simply made to vanish. But Rivera managed to charm Calles's education minister, José Manuel Puig Casauranc, who called Rivera the "philosopher of the brush," and he was kept on the government payroll. Rivera was a master of what is now known as networking. He made connections with friends and supporters all over the world, people who helped him obtain commissions and show his work to the public, just as sculptor Ralph Stackpole helped him to get the San Francisco commissions.

When Kahlo and Rivera arrived in San Francisco, they moved into Stackpole's large studio on Montgomery Street in the city's art neighborhood. One of their neighbors, Lucille Blanch, an artist whose husband, Arnold Blanch, was teaching at the California School of Fine Arts, remembered Kahlo's shyness about her own work.

"Frida did not set herself up as an artist," Blanch said. "We were both painters yet we did not talk about art. She scintillated in her talk, made fun of everything and everybody, laughing at things sportively and perhaps snobbishly. She was very critical if she thought something was pretentious, and often laughed at San Franciscans."

Kahlo and Rivera were well covered by the press. They were news, although the reporters pretty much ignored Kahlo. They concentrated on Rivera, the controversial "wild man" from Mexico, who had come to shake up the American art scene.

Rivera became fascinated with the female tennis star Helen Wills and used her as a model in some of his paintings. While he was busy with his murals, Kahlo toured San Francisco. She was especially intrigued by Chinatown, and she wrote to a friend that the Chinese children were so beautiful. "Yes, they are really extraordinary. I would love to steal one so that you could see for yourself."

She was not altogether happy among Americans, however. "I do not like the gringo people," she wrote. "They are boring and they all have faces like unbaked rolls (especially the old women)."

Kahlo met the photographer Edward Weston, Tina Modotti's former lover, and he described her as "a little doll alongside Diego, but a doll in size only, for she is strong and quite beautiful, shows very little of her father's German blood. Dressed in native costume, even to huaraches [sandals], she causes much excitement on the streets of San Francisco. People stop in their tracks to look in wonder."

It was in San Francisco that Kahlo met Dr. Leo Eloesser, a well-known physician who specialized in bone surgery. While in San Francisco, Kahlo was hospitalized for a problem with her foot, and Dr. Eloesser took care of her. He became a life-long friend and medical adviser.

After a brief return to Mexico, Kahlo and Rivera returned to San Francisco, where Rivera began the mural for the California School of Fine Arts. Entitled *The Making of a Fresco*, it shows Rivera seated on a scaffold, his back to the viewer, painting a mural of a helmeted worker at the controls of a machine. Also in the painting are school officials and the school architect, Arthur Brown Jr., dressed in suits. Some San Franciscans were offended by the view of Rivera's ample backside facing the audience. The mural was a kind of joke, but some didn't think it was funny.

In June 1931, Kahlo and Rivera returned to Mexico, where the new president, Pascual Ortiz Rubio, wanted Rivera to continue work on the murals at the National Palace. The couple lived in the Casa Azul in Coyoacán while Rivera was building a new house for them in the San Angel section of Mexico City. It was actually two houses linked by a bridge, so that the two artists could have their privacy but still be together when they felt like it.

NEW YORK AND THE SOCIAL SCENE

Rivera went back to work on the National Palace murals, but, once again, he was interrupted, this time by an offer he couldn't refuse. The new Museum of Modern Art in New York wanted to give him a one-man show. The museum had presented only one other one-man show—for Henri Matisse. He was to exhibit 143 paintings, watercolors, and drawings, as well as 7 movable frescoes (wall or ceiling paintings made while the plaster is still wet).

Despite the frantic activity to prepare for the show, Kahlo and Rivera had time for a social life. They met many influential people who liked to associate with artists, including John D. and Abby Rockefeller and Lucienne and Suzanne Bloch, daughters of the Swiss composer Ernest Bloch.

Lucienne Bloch was fascinated by Rivera and at a dinner party spent hours talking to him. "I was very impressed with Diego's idea that machines were marvelous," she said. "All the artists I knew thought machines were terrible." Once in a while, she noticed that Kahlo was giving her dark looks. Finally, Kahlo came up to her and said, "I hate you!"

"I was very impressed," Bloch said. "This was my first contact with Frida and I loved her for it." The two women later became good friends. Bloch went to work for Rivera as an assistant and later married another assistant. When she had her first child, Kahlo was the godmother.

Although Kahlo went along with her husband's social activities, she had strong feelings about the divisions between rich and poor that she saw in the United States. She wrote to her friend Dr. Eloesser: "High society here turns me off and I feel a bit of rage against all these rich guys here, since I have seen thousands of people in the most terrible misery without anything to eat and with no place to sleep."

Rivera's show was a big success. It attracted more visitors than any previous show at the museum. The New York critics were very favorable. One critic said Rivera was "the most talked about man on this side of the Atlantic."

Kahlo began to feel better about New York after the show closed on January 27, 1932, and her husband had more time for her. They went to parties and met many new friends. Kahlo liked to explore Manhattan and enjoyed the movies, especially the films of the Marx Brothers, Three Stooges, and Laurel and Hardy. She saw *Frankenstein* more than once.

All this was soon to come to an end, however. Rivera received commissions to paint murals in Detroit. He looked forward to being in the city where the machine was king, but Kahlo would not be happy there.

The Perils of "Gringolandia"

The Riveras arrived in Detroit on April 21, 1932. *The Detroit News* reported that Kahlo wore a black silk brocade dress with corded shirrings at the round neck; a long dark-green embroidered silk shawl; high spindle-heeled slippers; heavy, dark uncut amber beads; and a jadeite necklace with carved pendants. That's how newsworthy the couple had become: Kahlo's every article of clothing was news. She called herself "Carmen" in Detroit because "Frida" sounded too German, and there was a growing anti-German feeling in the country with the rise of Adolf Hitler and the Nazis. Not only did Kahlo remain in the shadow of her famous husband, she couldn't even use her own name.

Rivera had accepted a commission to paint murals celebrating the Detroit auto industry. The president of the Ford Motor Company, Edsel Ford, agreed to pay $10,000 for murals approved by the Detroit Arts Commission, which Ford headed.

STRIKING OUT AGAINST ANTI-SEMITISM

Not long after stepping off the train in Detroit in 1932, the Riveras became involved in an old prejudice: anti-Semitism. They took up residence in the Wardell, a residential hotel across the street from the Detroit Institute of Arts. They soon discovered that the Wardell did not admit Jews. Rivera told the management that both he and Kahlo had Jewish blood and would have to leave.

The management was so upset that such a famous a couple would move out of their hotel that they offered to lower the rent. But Rivera demanded that the restriction against Jews be lifted or he and his wife would have to go. Not only did the management agree, they also reduced the rent from $185 to $100 a month. The Riveras had scored a victory for tolerance.

Then, at a dinner party given by automaker Henry Ford, the issue was raised again when Kahlo went up to the man whom she knew was a notorious anti-Semite and asked innocently, "Mr. Ford, are you Jewish?" Rivera thought that was uproariously funny. Ford's reaction was not recorded, but the old industrialist probably got a kick out of it because later he and Kahlo tore up the dance floor together.

Kahlo's remark to Henry Ford about Jews was just one of the ways that she expressed her displeasure with the snobbishness of the Grosse Pointe people. The society women made it clear they didn't approve of Kahlo's manner of dress. She got back at the capitalists' wives by talking to them about the glories of Communism and, in a Catholic household, made snide remarks about the Catholic Church. She even used vulgar language, pretending that she didn't know the meaning of the English words.

"What I did to those old biddies!" she would laugh later.

In a letter to Dr. Eloesser, Kahlo wrote, "This city seems to me like a shabby old village. I don't like it at all, but I am happy because Diego is working very happily here, and he has found a lot of material for his frescoes that he will do in the museum."

Rivera and Kahlo share a tender moment in 1932 in the interior court of the Detroit Institute of Arts, where Rivera was completing a mural. Kahlo's time in Detroit was marked with difficulties: She encountered anti-Semitism, had to hide her German ancestry, and suffered a miscarriage.

Kahlo's costumes were not always greeted with disdain. Rivera recalled how at one party all eyes were on her. Rivera always enjoyed seeing his wife the center of attention, never concerned that she was taking the limelight away from him.

While Rivera was fascinated by the factories and machines, "like a child with a new toy," Kahlo was discouraged by the shabbiness of much of Detroit, especially where the poor people lived. She noted that the poor in Mexico tended their homes with great care and had a sense of color that she didn't find in the dreary city.

PREGNANCY AND PAINTING

Kahlo found herself pregnant in Detroit, and she was determined to have the baby. But on the July 4, 1932, she was rushed to the Henry Ford Hospital with severe bleeding. She had lost the child after two months of pregnancy. She spent 13 days in the hospital and was filled with despair. "I wish I were dead," she cried. "I don't know why I have to go on living like this."

Out of this experience, she painted one of her masterpieces, *Henry Ford Hospital*. It is grim and surrealistic, showing her bleeding on a floating bed with red ribbons linked to six suspended objects, including a fetus, two spinal columns, a snail, a strange piece of machinery, and a woman's torso. Rivera was enthusiastic about the painting, and several paintings followed it. "Frida began work on a series of masterpieces which had no precedent in the history of art—paintings which exalted the feminine qualities of endurance, of truth, reality, cruelty, and suffering," he wrote later. "Never before had a woman put such agonized poetry on canvas as Frida did in Detroit."

KAHLO'S RETABLO COLLECTION

The word *retablo* is derived from the Latin *retro tabula*, which means "behind the altar." Unlike Spanish retablos, religious works placed behind church altars, the retablos popular in nineteenth-century Mexico were used to decorate family altars at home. They were often created by amateur artists who based their designs on images they observed in Mexican churches or in religious books. With Rivera's encouragement, Kahlo collected retablos, many of which can be found today at the Casa Azul in Coyoacán.

Another work at that time was *My Birth*, a frightening bit of surrealism in which Kahlo's mother, partially covered like a corpse, is shown giving birth to Frida, depicted as an enormous child emerging headfirst into the world. Kahlo was in full bloom as an artist, experimenting with other techniques, making lithographs, painting on tin, and even trying her hand at frescoes. One lithograph remains—*Frida and the Abortion*. It is a sad and potent portrait of a passive woman submitting to the various stages of pregnancy and the loss of her child. Her blood drips into the earth to fertilize a garden.

In her marriage to Rivera, Kahlo had at least two abortions and a miscarriage. "I lost three children," she wrote later in her life. "Paintings substituted for all this. I believe that work is the best thing." But her inability to have Rivera's child haunted her life, even though he made it clear he didn't want any more children.

At this time, Kahlo also painted *Self-Portrait on the Borderline Between Mexico and the United States*. She depicted the sun and the moon in the sky over the Mexican side of the painting and an American flag floating in smog on the U.S. side. (The sun and the moon were significant symbols to Kahlo, representing what Herrera calls "an eternal war between light and dark, the preoccupation in Mexican culture with the idea of duality: life-death, light-dark, past-present, day-night, male-female.") The painting illustrates her feelings that the United States was a colorless place of machinery and smoke, whereas Mexico was fertile and beautiful. It also showed how anxious she was to get back home.

DEATH IN THE FAMILY

Unfortunately, when Kahlo returned to Mexico, it was so that she could be with her mother during her final illness. Accompanied by her friend Lucienne Bloch, she traveled to Mexico by train and bus, a long, frustrating journey. On September 15, 1932, a week after Kahlo arrived in Coyoacán, her mother, Matilde Calderón de Kahlo, died. Kahlo was

RETABLOS AND EX-VOTOS

Some of Kahlo's work was influenced by Mexican retablo and ex-voto tradition. Popular throughout the nineteenth century, retablos were paintings of saints or deities on small, rectangular pieces of tin. Also religious in nature (and typically painted on an inexpensive material), ex-votos depicted Jesus Christ, the Virgin Mary, or any of the numerous Catholic saints helping people in their times of need. Very often, the religious figures were seen assisting somebody who was sick or dying. The images were intended to demonstrate thanks and appreciation, and they were usually accompanied by a short written explanation of the miracle's circumstances.

Kahlo's 1926 pencil sketch *The Accident*, which shows her lying in the wake of her trolley mishap, is an early example of the influence of ex-votos on her work. *Henry Ford Hospital,* which likewise includes date and location inscribed on the hospital bed, is also reminiscent of this traditional form. Only where a traditional Mexican ex-voto might have portrayed Jesus Christ looking over the painting's subject, Kahlo has instead depicted floating, symbolic objects. In her 1954 painting *Marxism Will Give Health to the Sick*, it is Karl Marx who is portrayed in lieu of a religious savior.

By painting on sheets of metal in a style recalling retablos, Kahlo connected herself to the Mexican cultural traditions that preceded her. She also conveyed that she was an artist of the people, since the materials she chose to work with were comparatively inexpensive.

heartbroken, but she had to think about her father, Guillermo, who was not well either and had lapses of memory.

Kahlo stayed in Mexico for five weeks, then returned to Detroit on October 21.

BACK TO DETROIT

Kahlo didn't recognize Rivera when she got off the train in Detroit. He had dieted and lost a lot of weight. His old clothes didn't fit him anymore, and he had to borrow a suit from a friend to meet his wife. "Finally, acknowledging my identity," he wrote later, "she embraced me and began to cry."

Rivera's weight loss and the long hours he was putting in on the mural took a toll on his moods. He became irritable and rarely had time for his wife. He was racing against time because he had accepted more commissions—one for a mural in Rockefeller Center in New York City and one on the theme of Machinery and Industry at the 1933 World's Fair in Chicago. In addition, Rivera was active in the Mexican community of Detroit, especially in arranging transportation for Mexican workers who had come to the United States in the 1920s for work but who now, in the Great Depression, had no jobs and wanted to go home.

Meanwhile, Kahlo produced another self-portrait, this one also painted on metal. It shows a spirited and pretty Frida dressed in a white blouse with lace trim and a string of jade beads around her neck.

At this time, Kahlo was interviewed by a reporter for *The Detroit News*, who wrote that people might be surprised to discover that the wife of the famous muralist also "dabbles" in art. "No," she is quoted as saying, "I didn't study with Diego. I didn't study with anyone. I just started to paint." Although she made jokes and needled the interviewer, what she said about her origins as a painter was accurate. She never studied art formally and never apprenticed herself to anyone. Her talent was hers alone and therefore unique.

MIXED REACTIONS TO RIVERA'S MURAL

Rivera's Detroit mural caused considerable controversy. It was unveiled on March 13, 1933, and there was an immediate storm of criticism from certain circles. Church people thought it was sacrilegious; conservatives found it communistic; others thought it was obscene. Some civic leaders threatened to wash it off the wall. The dispute was broadcast over radio and written about in newspapers. The general public, however, especially

While living in Detroit, Kahlo painted *Self-Portrait on the Borderline Between Mexico and the United States* (*above*), which expressed her ambivalence about the United States. The painting depicts contrasting symbols of Mexico—great Aztec architectural ruins and forces of nature—and the United States—mighty skyscrapers and industrial smokestacks.

the workers who toiled making Ford automobiles and who were depicted in the painting, loved it. In fact, they took turns guarding it. And Edsel Ford, who had commissioned the work, defended Rivera. "I admire Rivera's spirit," he said. "I really believe he was trying to express his idea of the spirit of Detroit."

On a bitterly cold day in March of 1933, Rivera, Kahlo, and Rivera's assistants arrived in Grand Central Station in New York to begin his most controversial work of all.

FIGHTING ROCKEFELLER IN NEW YORK

Kahlo was happy to be back in New York. She had many friends there, but she also appreciated the fact that New York was a port city. She had felt trapped in Detroit, but in New York she could dream about hopping on a boat to take her back to Mexico. Going home was a dream she would never lose as she made her way through the perils of "Gringolandia."

She and Rivera moved into the Barbizon-Plaza, and Rivera went to work in the RCA Building. Rivera was so well known by then that people paid to watch him work. Kahlo would visit him two or three times a week, usually in the evening when the paying guests had departed. She didn't paint much during this period. She spent her time wandering around Manhattan, enjoying the department stores, the shops in Chinatown, and discount shops that were then called dime stores.

"Frida would go through dime stores like a tornado," her friend Lucienne Bloch said. "Suddenly she would stop and buy something immediately. She had an extraordinary eye for the genuine and the beautiful. She'd find cheap costume jewelry and she'd make it look fantastic."

Kahlo didn't like the theater or concerts. She much preferred movies, such as Tarzan films. Once during a Tchaikovsky performance, she and Bloch acted like rude children, making drawings and paper birds and giggling loudly.

But things started to get serious for Rivera. For some reason, it hadn't occurred to the 25-year-old Nelson Rockefeller, son of John D. Rockefeller Jr., future governor of New York and future vice president of the United States, that it probably wasn't a good idea to hire an avowed Communist to paint a mural in New York City, the heart of capitalism. But Rockefeller had chosen the theme for the mural himself: Man at the Crossroads Looking with Hope and High Vision to the Choosing of a New and Better Future. His representatives had approved of Rivera's sketches. He had liked Rivera's Detroit mural. Everything seemed fine.

But the *New York World-Telegram* took a look at the mural when it was two-thirds complete and published a story on April 24 with this headline, "Rivera Paints Scenes of Communist Activity and John D. Jr. Foots the Bill." The newspaper observed that the predominant color of the mural was red, the color associated with Communism. And it seemed to imply the victory of Communism over capitalism.

Suddenly, Rivera and his mural were in trouble. Guards started showing up. Fights broke out between the guards and Rivera's assistants. When a photographer hired by Rivera tried to take pictures of the incomplete mural, he was thrown out of the building. Eventually, Bloch, with a camera hidden under her skirts, photographed it.

The final straw came when Rivera painted the face of Vladimir Lenin on what was supposed to be the figure of a labor leader. Rockefeller, still trying to make peace with his renegade painter, urged him to substitute the face of an unknown man for Lenin. Rivera, of course, refused. However, he did offer to balance Lenin by painting the face of Abraham Lincoln on another figure. Rockefeller didn't bother to reply. Instead, his rental manager, accompanied by 12 uniformed security guards, arrived at the building on May 9 and ordered Rivera to stop working. When the artist climbed down from his scaffolding, he was handed a check for $14,000, the remainder of what Rockefeller owed him on the $21,000 contract. The scaffolding was taken down and workers covered the mural with tar paper and a wooden screen.

The controversy raged. Mounted police had to be called when Rivera's supporters arrived to picket Rockefeller Center. Picketers also went to Rockefeller's home. They carried signs that read, "Save Rivera's Painting," and "We want Rockefeller with a rope around his neck! Freedom in art!" A group of artists and intellectuals, including some of the leading figures in art and literature of the time, petitioned Rockefeller to save the mural. Of course, Rockefeller had the final say.

Rivera got more bad news a few days later when his friend, architect Albert Kahn, who designed the General Motors

Building at the Chicago World's Fair, sent him a telegram saying his commission to paint the *Forge and Foundry* mural at the fair had been cancelled.

Kahlo had done everything she could think of to save the RCA mural. She wrote letters and attended protest meetings. A few months later, she ran into Nelson Rockefeller at the opening of Sergei Eisenstein's film, *Que Viva Mexico!* Rockefeller was cordial. "How are you, Frida?" he asked. She turned on her heel and marched off. However, Kahlo's enemies were usually only temporary ones. Seven years later in 1940, she ran into Rockefeller in Mexico when he was making arrangements for an exhibition, "Twenty Centuries of Mexican Art," at the Museum of Modern Art in New York. A photograph shows her sitting next to him at a luncheon.

COMMUNISM IN AMERICA

It's important to know that Communism had a strong appeal to some Americans who were suffering in the Great Depression. It seemed to them that the capitalist system of private ownership was not working and maybe it was time to try something else. Socialists wanted government ownership of the means of production, and Communists wanted the workers to be in charge. They believed that the government would eventually "wither away" under Communism, and that workers' groups would take over and everybody would live in peace and freedom. Many of those who got involved in Communism regretted it later when they discovered that the Soviet Union did not really have a Communist government under Joseph Stalin and that it was a ruthless dictatorship. Among those who fought against Stalin was Leon Trotsky, who would soon play an important role in the lives of Diego Rivera and Frida Kahlo.

HOMESICK IN NEW YORK

After the turmoil over the Rockefeller Center mural, Kahlo was anxious to go back to Mexico. She and Rivera fought long and loudly over the issue. He wanted to stay in New York, where he was a popular figure and was hailed wherever he went. But there was no glory for Kahlo in Manhattan. She had not been very creative there. Toward the end of their nine months in New York, she managed to start a painting, *My Dress Hangs There,* which she finished in Mexico. It is a sad piece of work, showing her empty Tehuana dress hanging on a ribbon stretched between two columns. On one of the columns is a toilet; on the other, a sports trophy. All around are images of the big city, including a poster of Mae West; churches (with the cross turned into a dollar sign); apartment and office buildings, including one on fire; and a trash can brimming with discarded junk and human parts and topped by a bloody hand. Looming over all is Federal Hall on Wall Street with the statue of George Washington in front. At the top is the port, showing the Statue of Liberty and a ship steaming away. No doubt, Kahlo pictured her homesick self on that boat.

Rivera had many friends in New York, including more than a few women. They followed him around like little puppies, and there's no doubt he became intimately involved with some. Kahlo not only yearned for Mexico, she wasn't feeling well. Her foot was partially paralyzed, and she hated the summer heat. She spent most of the day in the bathtub. Then November came, and the first snow fell. She was not looking forward to winter in New York. She yearned for her sunny homeland.

"New York is very pretty and I feel better here than in Detroit," she wrote to a friend, "but in spite of this, I am longing for Mexico."

Rivera, who always had a violent temper, once picked up a painting he had done of a Mexican desert landscape and shouted, "I don't want to go back to that!" He took a knife and cut it into shreds before the horrified eyes of Kahlo and some friends.

Nevertheless, on December 20, 1933, Kahlo finally got on board a ship like the one in her painting. She and Rivera returned to Mexico on the *Oriente.* Her return to Mexico was not to be the happy time that she had looked forward to.

"A Few Small Nips"

Kahlo was glad to be back in Mexico, but Rivera was not. He hadn't wanted to give up the attention and acclaim he was getting from the New York artists and intellectuals. He sulked for months, refused to work, and made Kahlo's life miserable by blaming her for dragging him back to Mexico against his will.

They moved into the double house in the San Angel section of Mexico City. It consisted of one big house for Rivera, including a high-ceilinged studio where he could not only work but entertain guests and exhibit his work for sale. Kahlo's house was smaller but also had a studio on the third floor with a big picture window. Rivera's house was painted pink; Kahlo's blue. A bridge linked the two houses.

RIVERA'S INFIDELITY
Kahlo was devastated to learn in 1934 that Rivera was having an affair with her younger sister, Cristina. Rivera had used

Cristina as a model for nudes in some of his murals and the relationship apparently developed from there. Possibly in reaction, Kahlo's first painting after that dry period was of a woman who had been stabbed to death by her boyfriend. It was entitled *A Few Small Nips* because when the killer went before the judge he said, "But I only gave her a few small nips." The gruesome painting shows the naked woman on a bed bleeding from numerous stab wounds while the killer stands over her. Some thought Kahlo saw herself in the brutalized woman. She, too, was suffering from the "small nips" that Rivera had been delivering for years by his bad behavior.

Rivera freely admitted that he treated women horribly. In his autobiography, he wrote: "If I loved a woman, the more I loved her, the more I wanted to hurt her. Frida was only the most obvious victim of this disgusting trait."

In some ways, the victim portrayed in *A Few Small Nips* is reminiscent of depictions of the dead Christ—arms slung to the side, a bloody palm exposed to the viewer. But Kahlo's painting is not solemn and self-pitying. Rather, as Herrera points out, the painting is emblematic of a kind of "black humor" traditional to Mexican popular culture. Through its shocking, unsettling imagery and spirit of caricature, or exaggeration, it evokes both "outrage and laughter."

In this sense, it draws from the work of a Mexican folk artist Rivera and Kahlo greatly admired, the influential José Guadalupe Posada (1851–1913). Posada was a prolific engraver and illustrator best known for his playful drawings of *calaveras* (skeletons), imagery today connected with the Mexican Day of the Dead celebration. He was also known for the darkly humorous scenes of horror he depicted in his broadsides, sheets of paper that were sold for pennies on streets and in outdoor markets.

During their first year back in Mexico, Kahlo and Rivera both endured physical problems. Rivera was still suffering the effects of the severe diet he went on in New York. In fact, a doctor ordered the man who once weighed 300 pounds to gain some weight. Kahlo had an appendectomy (surgery to remove her appendix) and had another abortion, this one after three months of pregnancy. Her right foot kept giving her trouble, and she finally agreed to have all five toes amputated.

Rivera finally got back to work on the frescoes at the National Palace. But he added insult to injury by painting Cristina and Frida in one scene, making Cristina a far more attractive and important figure than Frida.

Kahlo wrote to Dr. Eloesser, "I'm so down and discouraged now, so unhappy that I don't know how I'm going to go on. I realize that Diego is now more interested in her (Cristina) than me and I keep saying to myself that I have to be ready to accept compromises if I want him to be happy. But it's costing me so much to put up with all this and you can't imagine how I'm suffering." Even in her suffering, however, Kahlo's main concern still seemed to be how to make Rivera happy.

Kahlo continued for several years to depict in paintings her suffering over Rivera's affair with her sister. In *Memory* (1937), she shows herself standing next to an enormous bleeding heart on the ground. Dangling from ribbons are her colorful Tehuana costume on her left and her schoolgirl dress on her right. She herself is seen with short-cropped hair wearing a white skirt and blouse and jacket. In one hand, she is holding a liquor bottle, indicating that she was drinking heavily at the time. Kahlo did cut off her long, dark hair after discovering Rivera's relationship with her sister. But she let it grow back later.

Finally, Kahlo could not stand living with Rivera any longer and moved to an apartment on Avenida Insurgentes in the center of Mexico City. There, her old boyfriend, Alejandro Gómez Arias, visited her. He related later how Kahlo looked out the window and saw her sister Cristina getting gas in her car across the street.

"Look!" Gómez Arias quoted her as saying. "Come here! Why does she come and fill up her car in front of my house?"

Though the hurt of Rivera's betrayal continued for many years, it wasn't long before Kahlo forgave her sister. In fact, Cristina's children grew fond of their aunt, who helped pay for their schooling and music and dance lessons. Kahlo depicted the kids, Isolda and Antonio, in her 1940 painting *The Wounded Table*, in which they stand at the end of a table where Kahlo is seated.

Kahlo herself had romantic relationships with both men and women during this period. One intense affair was with the American sculptor Isamu Noguchi, who had come to Mexico to paint a mural. Noguchi said of Kahlo, "I loved her very much. She was a lovely person, absolutely marvelous person. Since Diego was well known to be a lady chaser, she cannot be blamed if she saw some men. In those days we all sort of, more or less, horsed around, and Diego did and so did Frida."

As if to prove that she had not lost her spirit, Kahlo and two women friends decided on an impulse to fly to New York. The flight was a disaster. The plane was forced to land several times, and they finished the trip by train. But she enjoyed being back in Manhattan, even if only for a short visit. It was there, according to her friend Bertram Wolfe, that Kahlo realized that, despite everything, it was Rivera she truly loved.

"As the flames of resentment died down," Wolfe wrote later, "she knew it was Diego she loved and that he meant more to her than the things that seemed to stand between them."

But Kahlo's romance with Leon Trotsky was the strangest of her relationships.

TROTSKY SEEKS ASYLUM

Trotsky was one of the leaders of the Russian Revolution in 1917. He and Vladimir Lenin were Bolsheviks, members of the revolutionary party that took over the country when Czar Nicholas II abdicated (left office). The Russian czar ruled the country like a king or emperor. Nicholas and his whole family were later killed by revolutionaries.

Kahlo welcomes Leon Trotsky (*second from right*) and his wife, Natalia, with the leader of the American Communist Committee, Max Schachtman, to Mexico. Trotsky and his wife took refuge in Kahlo's home. Kahlo, characteristically attracted to this powerful socialist leader, soon became entangled in an extramarital affair with Trotsky.

Trotsky had spent time in prison, including in Siberia, for earlier revolutionary activities. But he had escaped and lived in other countries at different times, including the United States. When Lenin returned to Russia from Germany, where he had been living, Trotsky joined him. Trotsky became Lenin's right-hand man. But after Lenin became ill in 1922, Joseph Stalin took power. Stalin and Trotsky turned into bitter enemies, and Stalin ordered him out of the country in 1929.

Trotsky had become friends with Diego Rivera, who put him and Lenin in two murals, the *Communist Unity Panel* at the New Workers School in New York, and *Man, Controller of the Universe* in Mexico City. So, when Trotsky had trouble finding a country that would take him in, Rivera intervened on his behalf with the Mexican government.

Rivera was a Trotskyite. He had met Stalin during a visit to the Soviet Union in 1927 and didn't like him. Rivera's fellow muralist, David Alfaro Siqueiros, was a Stalinist. The two got into violent arguments over the subject.

By this time, Lazaro Cardenas had been elected president of Mexico and sent the country back to its original revolutionary ideals—land and labor reforms. He kicked president Plutarco Elías Calles out of the country in 1936 because he was against such reforms.

Rivera used his influence with the new government to give Trotsky political asylum (safety) in Mexico. On November 9, 1937, Trotsky and his wife, Natalia, arrived in the harbor of Tampico aboard the oil tanker *Ruth*. Frida Kahlo, representing her husband, was among a party of dignitaries who met the couple. Rivera was in the hospital suffering from eye and kidney problems.

Trotsky was heavily guarded. He and his wife were aware that Stalin wanted him dead. In fact, Natalia was so terrified of possible killers that she refused to get off the ship until she saw some familiar faces. Trotsky was 57 years old, tall and energetic. He made friends wherever he went, and he easily charmed his hosts. They went to live in Kahlo's home in Coyoacán, where her father still lived. Kahlo's niece Isolda, writing in a book about her aunt published years later, in 2004, remembers Trotsky fondly: "[He] was a lovely man, highly disciplined, simple and affectionate. He was a darling with children. I used to cover him with kisses, and he never got annoyed."

Guillermo Kahlo was a little puzzled by the exiled Russian's stay in Mexico. He had never heard of Trotsky. He said to his daughter, "You esteem this person, don't you? I want to talk to him. I want to advise him not to get involved with politics. Politics are very bad." Later, Guillermo Kahlo moved in with his daughter Adriana.

But Trotsky wouldn't have taken Guillermo's advice. He was busy working on a biography of Lenin and forming an international commission to analyze the evidence used by Stalin to evict him from the Communist Party and the Soviet Union. The commission, headed by the American educator John Dewey, actually held a kind of trial in the Coyoacán house. It was attended by representatives of many countries and was covered by the press. At the end of the sessions, the commission declared Trotsky innocent of the charges against him.

While the trial was in session, guards stood outside the house, and windows facing the street were covered with adobe bricks. To make the house even more secure, Rivera bought the property next door, evicted the family that lived there, and connected the two dwellings. Rivera was now a member of the International Communist League, a Trotskyite organization.

AFFAIR WITH TROTSKY

Trotsky was very much interested in women. He tried to get close to Cristina, but she wanted no part of him. Kahlo, however, found the revolutionary hero very attractive, and he soon returned the affection. She was then 29 and, from photographs and her own self-portrait, quite beautiful. She and Trotsky began meeting in Cristina's home on Aguayo Street. Although Rivera seemed ignorant of the affair, Natalia Trotsky soon found out about it.

Trotsky moved to a farm near San Miguel Regla, about 80 miles (128 km) northeast of Mexico City. After a visit there with other friends, Kahlo broke off the relationship. Trotsky was upset and wrote her a nine-page letter telling her how much she meant to him. But it was all over.

On November 7, 1937, the anniversary of the Russian Revolution and Trotsky's birthday, Kahlo gave Trotsky a self-portrait, showing her standing between two curtains, holding in one hand a bouquet of flowers and in the other a note that says, "For Leon Trotsky with all love I dedicate this painting on the 7th of November, 1937. Frida Kahlo in San Angel, Mexico."

André Breton, the French surrealist poet, described Kahlo in the portrait after he saw it in Trotsky's study: "She has painted herself dressed in a robe of wings gilded with butterflies . . . We are privileged to be present . . . at the entry of a young woman endowed with all the gifts of seduction, one accustomed to the society of men of genius."

After the romance with Trotsky was over, Kahlo became more productive than she had been in years. She produced more paintings in 1937 and 1938 than she had during the entire eight years of her marriage.

The biographer Hayden Herrera points out that Kahlo's art had begun to correspond to her changing persona. Previous paintings like *Henry Ford Hospital* reflected specific incidents in her life. Her new works, however, reflected a sense of her inner self and her place in the world. The portrait she gave to Trotsky, like several other paintings from the period, exhibit a sense of confidence in her looks. Others like *My Nurse and I* and *Me and My Doll* reveal sorrow over the fact that she never conceived a child, Herrera suggests.

Kahlo considered *My Nurse and I* to be among her best paintings and indeed, its imagery is striking. The work depicts Kahlo as a baby, being breast-fed by her wet nurse. But in this scene, the baby Frida has an adult face. And the nurse has on a fearsome Teotihuacán stone mask, the kind traditionally placed over the faces of the dead at burial in ancient times.

Kahlo's own childhood inspired the piece. After her own mother fell ill shortly after her birth, Kahlo was nursed by an indigenous woman. The painting depicts a young Frida being cradled by the nurse, a suggestion that Kahlo's Indian heritage continues to nurture her even as an adult. The work is reminiscent both of certain Mexican ceramic art dating from the years 100 B.C. to A.D. 250, as well as a traditional type of Mexican Christian imagery known as Madonna Caritas. With its white raindrops falling from the sky and a natural backdrop that includes a giant leaf, a praying mantis, and a caterpillar turning into a butterfly, the painting also represents the natural world's interconnectedness.

And yet, there's something unsettling about that mask. Though Kahlo said she included it because she couldn't

THE DECEASED DIMAS

When Kahlo painted the somber *The Deceased Dimas*, she was following a Mexican artistic tradition of postmortem portraiture— that is, the painting of a person who has died. In this case, that person was Dimas Rosas, a Mexican youngster who died at the age of three because his father preferred to send his children to witch doctors instead of true medical professionals. Kahlo knew of Dimas through Rivera, who was probably the boy's godfather and likely used him and his siblings as models for his paintings.

Not surprisingly, Kahlo didn't adhere faithfully to convention. Where a typical postmortem portrait would have shown Dimas from the side, Kahlo painted from the perspective of someone staring down at the boy from just below his bare feet—a technique that brings the viewer into more intimate contact with the subject. He is dressed in a flowing robe like that worn by a holy figure and holds a flowering staff. He wears a cardboard crown, and yet rests on a straw mat that is a typical bed for Mexico's poor. The look on his face is haunting. Small droplets of blood trickle from his mouth. A small Christian postcard image rests on the pillow next to his head. Herrera notes that Kahlo had taken an atheist's view of death and that her original title for the painting, *Dressed Up for Paradise*, was meant to be sarcastic.

remember her nurse's face, Herrera suggests there is more to Kahlo's decision to include this detail. The mask represents ancient rituals involving human sacrifice, with Kahlo appearing to "be simultaneously protected by the nurse and offered as a sacrificial victim," she believes. One author, Andrea Kettenmann, raises the possibility that it could be indicative of a cool, distant relationship between the nurse and the baby—a lack of an emotional bond that could speak to Kahlo's feelings toward her own mother. Herrera points to the nurse's loose black hair and the mask's conjoined eyebrows as signs that the nurse is an ancestor or may represent another side of Kahlo's own self. As with Kahlo's other provocative paintings, there are many interpretations to be found.

With exhibits, sales, and visits to New York and Paris on the horizon, Kahlo's hard work between 1937 and 1938 paid off. Unfortunately, there was still tragedy to come.

KAHLO'S PAINTINGS SELL

Edward G. Robinson was the tough-guy actor of the American screen from the 1930s into the 1970s. One of his most famous roles was as the gangster in *Little Caesar* in 1930. But not many of his fans knew that he was an art collector with excellent taste. He was one of the first to buy Frida Kahlo's paintings.

It was Rivera who arranged for Robinson to see Kahlo's art when the actor and his wife, Gladys, were visiting Mexico in the summer of 1938. "I kept about 28 paintings hidden," Kahlo wrote later. "While I was on the roof terrace with Mrs. Robinson, Diego showed him my paintings and Robinson bought four of them from me for $200 each." She suddenly realized that she could make money selling her art. "For me it was such a surprise that I marveled and said: 'This way I am going to be able to be free, I'll be able to travel and do what I want without asking Diego for money.'"

Earlier that year, some of Kahlo's paintings were included in a group show at the University Gallery in Mexico City.

Kahlo's self-portrait with her monkey was one of 30 paintings shown at her first gallery exhibition in October 1938. A. Conger Goodyear, the president of the Museum of Modern Art, loved Kahlo's painting so much that, when he missed out on purchasing it, Kahlo produced another one specifically for him.

Someone who saw them there told Manhattan gallery owner Julien Levy about them. He wrote to Kahlo and said he was interested in showing her work at his gallery. She sent him some photographs of her paintings, and he wrote back saying he wanted to show 30 of her works that October. Ever modest about her paintings, Kahlo later told a friend, "I don't know what they see in my work. Why do they want me to have a show?" But she accepted the invitation.

Kahlo and Rivera drew up a list of important people to invite to the exhibit. It included some of the more important and famous people in the arts, business, and educational circles. Among them were Nelson Rockefeller and his father John D. Rockefeller Jr. Obviously, the Riveras didn't hold grudges, at least when it came to possible purchasers of Kahlo's art.

Kahlo went alone to New York. André Breton, who insisted that Kahlo was a fellow surrealist, had written a glowing introduction to the show for the catalogue. The fact that it was printed in the original French annoyed some people. At any rate, Kahlo did not consider herself a surrealist. Surrealist artists were known for distorting reality into dream-like shapes and images. Kahlo, who didn't link herself with any school of art, considered her paintings to be her own unique expression.

"They thought I was a surrealist," she once said, "but I wasn't. I never painted dreams. I painted my own reality."

But while the New York show was proceeding, the surrealist Breton was arranging an exhibit for her in Paris.

A reviewer for *Time* magazine wrote of the New York exhibit: "Little Frida's pictures, mostly painted in oil on copper, had the daintiness of miniatures, the vivid reds and yellows of Mexican tradition and the playfully bloody fancy of an unsentimental child."

About half of Kahlo's paintings sold. A. Conger Goodyear, president of the Museum of Modern Art, fell in love with Kahlo's painting of herself with her monkey, Fulang-Chang.

But it had been sold to someone else. So Kahlo sat in her hotel room at the Barbizon-Plaza and produced another picture of herself with her monkey just for Goodyear. Kahlo loved animals and had many pets, including several monkeys and parrots. She often painted herself with these creatures. Some have suggested this was because of both her loneliness and her desire for children.

Aside from the painting Goodyear commissioned and some drawings in her sketchbook, Kahlo did not produce much art while in Manhattan. She didn't spend a lot of time at the city's museums or bars, due to the difficulty she had walking. But with Rivera in Mexico, Kahlo indulged in her freedom, enjoying the seductive effect she had on men. She had romantic relationships with the New York gallery owner Levy as well as Nickolas Muray, a Hungarian-born photographer who achieved great success in the United States.

Kahlo most likely began having an affair with Muray in Mexico, and if her correspondence was any indication of the extent of her love for him, it was indeed intense. "I miss every movement of your being, your voice, your eyes, your hands, your beautiful mouth, your laugh so clear and honest," she wrote from Paris in February 1939. Kahlo wrote several letters to Muray in English. In another, she said "Nick I adore you so much. I need you so, that my heart hurts . . ."

Despite all of her relationships with other men, Kahlo still loved Diego Rivera above all and worried about him constantly, according to Herrera. In fact, she was reluctant to go to Paris for the exhibit André Breton had organized because she didn't want to leave Rivera alone in Mexico.

KAHLO TAKES PARIS

Rivera wrote to her in New York: "I don't want you for my sake to lose the opportunity to go to Paris. Take from life all which she gives you, whatever it may be, provided it is interesting and can give you some pleasure."

Kahlo arrived in Paris in January 1939. The start of World War II was only months away, and the world was on edge. In addition, the Paris exhibition started out as a disaster. For one thing Breton, whom Kahlo didn't really like very much, botched the organizing of the show. Finally, the artist Marcel Duchamp, whom Kahlo said was the only one "who has his feet on the earth," took over. He found a gallery for the show, which was called Mexique. But Kahlo became ill with a kidney infection and had to be hospitalized. She wrote to Nikolas Muray that she was about to get out of Paris "before I get nuts myself."

She stayed, however, and the show opened March 10 at the Pierre Colle gallery. Her paintings were well received by the critics. And the Louvre, the foremost French museum of art, purchased one of her self-portraits, *The Frame*. Rivera wrote later that the Russian artist Wassily Kandinsky "was so moved

THE SUICIDE OF DOROTHY HALE

An example of Kahlo's independence as an artist came when the playwright Claire Booth Luce, wife of Henry Luce, who was the founder of *Time* magazine, asked Kahlo to paint a remembrance of her friend Dorothy Hale, who had committed suicide. Luce wanted a nice, warm painting that she could give to Hale's mother. But what Kahlo produced was so shocking, Luce couldn't even look at it. It showed Hale plunging from a tall building and lying bloody on the ground. With its depiction of a disaster, an angel, and a description of the event at the bottom of the painting, Kahlo's work brings to mind the Mexican style of ex-voto painting.

The Suicide of Dorothy Hale might have been a masterpiece, but it certainly wasn't what Luce had in mind. She had it locked away for decades, and no one saw it until a friend of Luce's donated it to the Phoenix Art Museum.

by Frida's paintings that, right before everyone in the exhibition room, he lifted her in his arms and kissed her cheeks and brow while tears of sheer emotion ran down his face." Although Rivera was not there, he got the information about the show secondhand. He also wrote that Pablo Picasso "sang the praises of Frida's artistic and personal qualities. From the moment he met her until she left for home, Picasso was under her spell."

That was probably true. Picasso gave Kahlo a pair of tiny tortoiseshell earrings in the shape of hands with gold cuffs and taught her a Spanish song. She used the earrings in paintings and enjoyed singing the song for friends.

Kahlo became something of a celebrity within Parisian artistic circles and attracted wide attention with her Tehuana costumes. In fact, Elsa Schiaparelli, the well-known Italian designer, created a dress based on Kahlo's outfits called La Robe Madame Rivera for fashionable Parisians. And Kahlo's hands, with her flashy jade and silver rings on her fingers, appeared on the cover of *Vogue.*

But Kahlo was anything but impressed with the Parisian artistic and intellectual culture she encountered. "You have no idea the kind of bitches these people are," she wrote to Muray. "They sit for hours on the 'cafes' warming their precious behinds, and talk without stopping about 'culture' 'art' 'revolution' and so on and so forth, thinking themselves the gods of the world, dreaming the most fantastic nonsenses, and poisoning the air with theories and theories that never come true."

Meanwhile, Rivera and Trotsky had a falling out in Mexico. They disagreed heatedly over political matters, and Rivera resigned from the Trotskyite Fourth International. Trotsky even wrote to Kahlo, seeking her help in healing their differences. She did not respond.

Strangely, Kahlo met the man who would kill Trotsky. While in Paris, she ran into Ramon Mercader, who was also known as Jacques Mornard. He made a pass at her, which she rebuffed. She related later that Mercader, who pretended to be a Trotskyite, asked her to find him a house near Trotsky in Mexico. She told him to find his own house. Mercader was actually an agent of the Soviet secret service, GPU, and he had been assigned by Stalin to kill Trotsky, which he did on August 20, 1940. After Trotsky's death, when Kahlo became a devotee of Joseph Stalin, she articulated a much less flattering opinion of her lover, telling an interviewer Trotsky was a coward and had stolen money from her, which wasn't true. "He irritated me from the time that he arrived with his pretentiousness, his pedantry because he thought he was a big deal," she was quoted as saying.

Kahlo's stay in Paris had its ups and downs, but she basically enjoyed the attention she received from some of the leading lights of the Parisian art world. Actually, the lights

WHAT THE WATER GAVE ME

Though Kahlo rejected the term "surrealist" to describe her work, her 1938 painting *What the Water Gave Me* is rich with the type of unexpectedly paired, symbolic imagery found in surrealist paintings that came out of Europe. The painting shows Kahlo's legs and feet as they would appear if she was lying in a bathtub. On the water's surface are a variety of images, including those of her parents on their wedding day, the Empire State Building jutting from an erupting volcano, a Tehuana dress, and a naked, drowned Kahlo with a tightrope wrapped around her neck. But unlike European surrealists who sought to portray an escape from reality, Kahlo's symbolism was more autobiographical and straightforward. Kahlo apparently talked to Julien Levy about the meaning of this work, which held special importance to her. "It's quite explicit," Levy once explained. "It is an image of passing time. She indicated, for one thing, that it was about time and childhood games and the sadness of what had happened to her in the course of her life."

of France were soon to go out. World War II began on September 1, 1939, when Germany invaded Poland. They were not to go back on until the liberation of Paris in 1945. But Kahlo escaped all that by returning to Mexico. She left Le Havre, France, for Mexico on March 25 by ship. Not long after her arrival, Rivera told her he wanted a divorce.

DIVORCE

No one was sure why Diego Rivera suddenly wanted to divorce his wife. There was speculation that he had found out about her affair with Trotsky. There was also speculation that she had found out about his possible affair with the American movie actress Paulette Goddard, who lived for a time in a hotel across from his San Angel studio. There is a photograph showing him and the Hungarian painter Irene Bohus painting portraits of Goddard. There was also a rumor that Rivera planned to marry Bohus.

As often happened to Kahlo, she and her husband's mistress, Paulette Goddard, became friends. She painted a still life, *The Flower Basket,* for Goddard in 1941.

Whatever the cause of the divorce, the couple began the proceedings on September 19, 1939. Kahlo's old school friend Manuel Gonzalez Ramirez was her lawyer, and the divorce was made final the next month. Rivera told the press that the divorce was only a matter of "legal convenience." He told *Time* magazine that it was done "in order to improve Frida's legal position . . . purely a matter of legal convenience in the spirit of modern times." He added that there was "no change in the magnificent relations between us."

Kahlo herself told a reporter that there were "intimate reasons, personal causes, difficult to explain," for the divorce. Rivera continued to honor his ex-wife when talking to reporters. He said he considered her "among the five or six most prominent modernist painters."

Meanwhile, Kahlo's art career was blooming. On the day that the divorce papers came through, she had nearly finished

The Two Fridas expresses Kahlo's anguish over her marital crisis. The Mexican Frida on the right holds a portrait of Rivera. Her heart is connected to that of the European Frida on the left, who is without Rivera. A surgical clamp on her exposed artery prevents her from bleeding to death.

one of her most famous paintings, *The Two Fridas*. The two figures of herself sit side by side. One is dressed as a European lady; the other in her famous Tehuana costume. They are holding hands. In both figures, the hearts are exposed and linked by a blood-filled artery. The European figure holds a clamp and is trying to stop the flow of blood that threatens to destroy them both. Drops of blood drip on her white skirt. The Tehuana Kahlo holds a miniature painting of Diego Rivera as a child. *The Two Fridas* was one of her biggest works, at 67 by 67 inches (170 cm).

That painting and *The Wounded Table* were exhibited at the International Surrealism Exhibition organized by the Gallery of Mexican Art in Mexico City in January 1940. In *The Wounded Table,* Kahlo is seated at a long table on what looks like a theater stage, accompanied by her niece and nephew, Isolda and Antonio Kahlo; her pet fawn, El Granizo (hail); a Judas figure (a figure symbolizing evil forces); a pre-Columbian (produced before the arrival of Christopher Columbus in the New World in 1492) idol; and a skeleton. Blood is dripping everywhere, and the painting is seen as a message to Rivera, showing how he has wounded her. The Judas figures were a Mexican tradition. They were made of papier-mâché and were meant to be burned as effigies (representations of despised figures) during the season of Lent.

The Two Fridas was exhibited later in New York in the Museum of Modern Art's exhibition Twenty Centuries of Mexican Art. One art critic who saw the painting commented that "the most recent of Rivera's ex-wives" was a "painter apparently obsessed by an interest in blood." It was sold to the Institute of Fine Arts in Mexico but not until seven years later. *The Wounded Table* had a more interesting history. It was exhibited in Warsaw, Poland, in 1955, then reportedly sent to the Soviet Union as a gift from the Mexican Communist Party. What happened to it after that is not known.

Artist of
the Casa Azul

Someone once asked Kahlo why she painted so many self-portraits. She replied, "Because I am alone." Many of Kahlo's paintings depict her as wounded. Some reflect the streetcar accident that left her damaged; others seem to refer to the wounds inflicted on her by men and life in general. One is *Self-Portrait with Thorn Necklace and Hummingbird,* in which the thorns cut into her neck as her monkey and cat look on. A dead hummingbird dangles from the necklace. Herrera suggests the bird's lifeless body probably refers to the fact that Kahlo "felt 'murdered by life.'" Nevertheless, hummingbirds also held a special place in Mexican culture, as "magic charms to bring luck in love," Herrera writes.

The painting is also emblematic of Kahlo's use of Christian imagery—her necklace's thorns calling back to the biblical story of Jesus's crucifixion, in which a crown of thorns was placed on the savior's head. By casting herself with thorns, Kahlo presents herself as a martyr.

An even more gruesome painting is *The Broken Column.* It is another self-portrait, this one showing her with nails driven into her face and body. Kahlo's exposed spine is bound together with straps. Tears pour from her eyes. The cloth on her hips is reminiscent of Christ's winding sheet, the garment used to wrap his corpse. Says Herrera: "Frida displays her wounds like a Christian martyr, a Mexican Saint Sebastian, she used physical pain, nakedness, and sexuality to bring home the message of her spiritual suffering."

Besides such gory works, Kahlo was capable of producing beautiful portraits, including a sensitive one of Doña Rosita Morillo Safa, an elderly woman shown knitting with flowering cacti behind her. Kahlo was commissioned to paint that portrait by Safa's son, Eduardo Morillo Safa, an engineer and diplomat, who also paid her to paint portraits of other members of his family, all beautifully done.

Many of Kahlo's still lifes, such as the painting of flowers that she did for Paulette Goddard and one called *Life, How I Love You,* of plump melons and other fruit, capture her unique sense of beauty and reverence for life.

Many of Kahlo's self-portraits over the years show her with closely cropped hair. That's because every time she got angry at Rivera, who loved her long, black tresses, she chopped them off.

Kahlo's health deteriorated after her divorce. In addition to being upset by the murder of Trotsky and the fact that police questioned her about it because she had known the killer, she was drinking heavily and was in constant pain from her old injuries and sicknesses. In September 1940, she flew to San Francisco for treatment by her old friend Dr. Eloesser. He prescribed rest, a special diet, and other therapies and told her to stop drinking. Her health improved greatly after that visit.

While in San Francisco, she showed her work at the Golden Gate International Exhibition.

REMARRIAGE TO RIVERA

Eloesser also urged Rivera and Kahlo to get back together. On Rivera's fifty-fourth birthday, December 8, 1940, they were married again. Kahlo was 33.

The transition back to married life wouldn't have been a perfectly smooth one, in part because of the fact that Kahlo had been romantically involved with a 25-year-old Jewish refugee from Germany by the name of Heinz Berggruen. He was a friend of Rivera, who had introduced Berggruen to Kahlo when she was in the hospital. According to Berggruen, he visited Kahlo at her hospital bedside every day for a month. They had even spent time together in New York, with Berggruen traveling a day ahead of her.

Berggruen's memories of Kahlo are a testament to the artist's sly sense of humor. When he and Kahlo would read the morning newspaper, for example, Kahlo would laugh at the photographs that typically accompanied columnists' articles. "Look at those crazy heads!" she'd say. As Herrera explains: "She could not imagine why the newspaper bothered to print photographs of these often unattractive faces." Likewise, Kahlo laughed at the automatic breakfast chute at her New York City hotel room. "God, these Americans," she said. "Everything in this country is mechanized, even breakfast!"

Alas, it was Rivera who would be Kahlo's long-term partner, but despite her remarriage, she was determined to live an independent life. She moved back to the Casa Azul in Coyoacán, while Rivera remained in the double house in San Angel.

Kahlo hung a skeleton next to her bed and gave it a handshake and affectionate greeting every morning. She also kept a fetus in formaldehyde in a jar on her bookshelf. She told visitors it was her own stillborn child. She might have been kidding. She had an eccentric sense of humor. She also had a large collection of pre-Columbian figures, art objects, curios, dolls, and toys. Kahlo always asked friends who were going to take trips to bring her back a toy. Huge Judas figures were placed in various rooms and on the patio. There is a photograph of her and Rivera standing with one of these figures, which appears to be about 12 feet tall (3.6 meters).

Rivera added a wing to the Casa Azul. It was made of volcanic rock and decorated with stone mosaics. The largest room was Kahlo's studio. Her many pets, including monkeys, birds, her deer, a dog, and other creatures, could run freely through the house. Her bedroom was a remarkable place. The bed, in which she spent a great deal of time because of her illnesses, had an overhead mirror. The headboard was completely covered with photographs of family and friends. There were portraits of Karl Marx and Friedrich Engels, whose ideas led to the development of Communism, as well as those of Lenin, Stalin, and Mao Tse-tung, the Communist leader of China. She still used the wooden easel her mother had rigged up for her years ago to paint while lying in bed.

Kahlo's father, Guillermo, died in 1941. His death was one more blow in a life that had seen many setbacks and disappointments. Nevertheless, during the 1940s, she painted a series of remarkable self-portraits. Critics point out that her paintings from this period were bigger than the ones she had done in the previous decade and were probably intended to appeal to a wider audience.

Self-Portrait as a Tehuana (Diego in My Thoughts) shows her in an elaborate Tehuana headdress with a picture of Rivera on her forehead. A similar painting, entitled simply *Self-Portrait,* shows her in a similar finely wrought headpiece with tears dripping from her eyes.

The hummingbird shows up again in a 1946 self-portrait, its outstretched wings form her dramatic eyebrows. Another from 1943 has her posed against a riot of vines and leaves with a picture of a skull and bone on her forehead. It is entitled *Thinking of Death.* A portrait from 1949 shows a much darker

Rivera watches over Kahlo's shoulder as she paints a self-portrait.

image of Kahlo with a larger picture of Rivera on her forehead. This time he has a third eye in the middle of his own forehead. (A third eye signifies wisdom.) Her rich black hair swirls about her neck. And once again tears are dripping from her eyes. It is entitled *Diego and I*. She also painted numerous other self-portraits with her various pets, mostly monkeys and parrots.

Speaking to the art critic Antonio Rodríguez, she explained why she expressed herself through her art. "Since the accident changed my path, and many other things, I was not permitted to fulfill the desires which the whole world considers normal, and nothing seemed more natural than to paint what had not been fulfilled," she told him in an interview. "I have painted little, and without the least desire for glory or ambition, but with the conviction that, before anything else, I want to give myself pleasure and then, that I want to be able to earn my living with my craft . . . many lives would not be enough to paint the way I would wish and all that I would like."

Kahlo was not able to paint as quickly as she would have liked, in part because of her physical disabilities. Though Rivera encouraged her and even withheld money in hopes that it would make his wife more productive, Kahlo was unable to produce another body of work that could be displayed at another one-woman exhibition.

Claire Booth Luce was not the only one who was unhappy upon receiving a commissioned painting from Kahlo. Mexican president Avila Camacho paid her to do *Still Life*, but turned it down when he saw it. It is an image of a grotesquely overripe melon, its innards exposed, surrounded by other fruit and a large butterfly. Kahlo often used overripe or broken fruit to represent her own body, which had been cut and torn over the years by accidents and surgery.

Still, Kahlo was becoming famous. In 1942, her paintings were included in an exhibition at New York's Museum of Modern Art entitled Twentieth-Century Portraits. Her work was also included in a New York exhibition of 31 women artists at Peggy Guggenheim's Art of This Century Gallery in January 1943, and in an exhibit of Mexican art at the Philadelphia Museum of Art that same year. Her portrait of Marucha Lavin, a circular work 25 inches in diameter (63.5 cm), was included in a group show at the Benjamin Franklin Library in Mexico City entitled A Century of the Portrait in Mexico, 1830–1942.

In 1943, Kahlo and Rivera taught art at the Education Ministry's School of Painting and Sculpture, known as La Esmeralda. On her first day at the school, Kahlo asked the students what they wanted to paint. They asked her to pose for them. One student, Guillermo Monroy, gave possibly the best description of what Kahlo was like at that time:

> Frida was there in front of us, amazingly still. Her hands, placed one of top of the other, were elegant and bedecked with rings. Her beautifully manicured fingernails were long and lacquered with bright red polish. Her silky black hair was criss-crossed on top of her head in meticulous braids, beautifully decorated in the center with a tiny bunch of gaudy magenta bougainvillea. Her filigree earrings were two small suns made of gold. Smooth skin, firm and cool. Dark, restless eyes seeing beyond earth and sky, black eyebrows joining to form the delicate wings of a bird. The freshest of smiles flowering on her red lips. Was it any wonder that many men were attracted to her over the years?

Kahlo wanted her students to go their own way in art. She rarely looked over their shoulders. She encouraged them to go out in the street to find subjects to paint.

"We all went to the markets, the factories, the countryside, we mixed with the people," Monroy said. "Frida told us that direct contact with life and participation in it, not as mere spectators, but as socially active citizens, would open new artistic horizons and greatly enrich our aesthetic and human sensitivity."

Kahlo was a popular teacher, and many of her students continued to study with her at the Casa Azul in Coyoacán when she was unable to make it to school. Four of her most devoted students were known as Los Fridos, in honor of their teacher.

Meanwhile, Rivera was back to work at the National Palace, this time painting panels of early Mexican civilizations.

He frequently included Kahlo in his murals. He also worked on a mural at the Institute of Cardiology, a two-wall fresco on the theme of religion versus science.

Kahlo's health gradually deteriorated through the 1940s, but in many ways the five years after her remarriage were possibly the happiest and most productive of her life. In 1946, she went to New York for surgery on her spine, which was probably botched and only added to her pain.

FINAL PAINTINGS

In 1942, as most of the rest of the world was torn by war, Rivera launched a project to build a sort of temple-museum to house his collection of treasures of Mexico's ancient history. It was also meant to be a ranch where he and Kahlo could be independent of a world they both saw as gradually going mad. They would live there, raise animals and their own fruits and vegetables, and be self-sufficient.

It was called Anahuacalli, and it turned out to be a strange, gloomy stone mausoleum-like structure set on a lava bed in

ROOTS

Kahlo's painting *Roots* is an homage to the volcanic earth where Anahuacalli stands. It features her body literally planted to the ground, with green leafy branches extending from her front and back. Observers have pointed out that the painting reveals how Kahlo, unable to bear children, wished to be connected to nature and the natural cycles of life. Herrera notes that the painting is "like a reversal of (or counterpart to) *My Nurse and I*. In the earlier painting, Kahlo depicted herself as an infant being nourished by her wet nurse's plant-like breast. *Roots*, on the other hand, shows Kahlo to be the one providing the plant its sustenance. In May 2006, *Roots* made history at the Sotheby's auction in New York City, when the painting sold for $5.6 million.

the Pedregal (stony ground) district near Coyoacán. Kahlo and Rivera never lived there and probably never planted anything there either, but Kahlo became as passionate about Anahuacalli as her husband. She contributed her own money to help build it and tried without success to get the Mexican government to chip in. It was finally opened to the public as a museum in 1964, long after both were dead.

As Kahlo's health continued to worsen in the 1940s, her fame spread. The Casa Azul was visited by people from all walks of life—show business, the arts, politics, and business. Even the Rockefellers came by, as did the famous dancer Josephine Baker and the Mexican film star Dolores del Rio. The visitors always got a delicious meal and were treated to Kahlo's unquenchable good humor. Even later, when confined to a wheelchair, she made people feel good by just being in their presence. Kahlo's family, however, was less than charmed by their famous relative. Her mother's sisters refused to visit her and would not let their children go to the house. After all, as far as they were concerned, the Riveras were living in sin. They were not married in the church *and* they were Communists. Her aunts actually sprinkled holy water on the sidewalk outside the "house of sin." But the two children of Kahlo's sister Cristina, Isolda and Antonio, were good company and also appeared in at least one of Aunt Frida's paintings. Every year, Kahlo held *posadas,* the traditional Christmas season parties, with piñatas for the children to break, fireworks, and colorful decorations and food. In 1946, Kahlo received the National Prize of Arts and Sciences from the Education Ministry. It carried a 5,000 peso prize. It was awarded for her painting *Moses.* She painted it after reading Freud's *Moses and Monotheism.* It is an unusual work for her, somewhat resembling Rivera's mural art. It is crowded with images—a snail; a skeleton; and images of great figures from history, including Jesus, Karl Marx, Gandhi, Napoleon, and Stalin; as well as nudes; Greek, Egyptian, and Aztec gods and goddesses; a fetus; and gnarled trees—all surrounding the infant Moses floating in a basket on the Nile under what looks like a boiling sun. Rivera usually crowded his murals with images, mostly of people in action, but it was unusual for Kahlo to jam so much into her paintings. *Moses* is also one of her largest paintings—30 by 24 inches (76.2 by 60.9 cm).

Kahlo began keeping her diary some time around 1944, when she 37 years old. She wrote in a red leather journal that a friend had bought for her in New York City. Kahlo's friend hoped the journal would comfort the artist when she wasn't feeling well. For Kahlo, such times were regrettably common.

In June 1946, Frida and Cristina flew to New York where Frida underwent a bone graft operation at the Hospital for Special Surgery. Four of her vertebrae were fused, and a metal rod was inserted to strengthen her spine. There was some evidence that the doctors fused the wrong vertebrae. She was in severe pain and required massive doses of morphine. Taking drugs, as well as drinking large amounts of alcohol, became a daily procedure in her final years. But Kahlo continued painting. She finished *Tree of Hope, Stay Strong* that year. It shows her in her Tehuana costume standing guard over another Frida, lying on a gurney (stretcher) with deep wounds in her back. The same year, she painted *The Little Deer,* a picture of a deer with Kahlo's head, pierced and bleeding from many arrows. The next year, Kahlo painted *Self-Portrait with Loose Hair,* in which the famously, saucy Kahlo now looks tired and drawn.

One of Kahlo's most amazing paintings at this time was *The Love Embrace of the Universe, the Earth (Mexico), Diego, Me and Senor Xolotl* (a pet deer). It shows her holding a naked Diego Rivera (with a large third eye), curled up like a child, in the embrace of huge arms, one dark and one light. Many of her later paintings depicted a dark and light world, signifying life and death.

Strangely, Kahlo painted a portrait of her father in 1951, 10 years after his death, with his camera beside him. She painted it while she was recovering from another bone graft operation, this one in the ABC Hospital in Mexico City and which required a year's recuperation. She no doubt used the easel her mother had erected over her bed so she could paint lying down. Kahlo painted a picture of herself in a wheelchair next to a portrait of Dr. Juan Farill, who did the bone graft. She is holding a painter's palette covered by a large heart. She often used the heart in her paintings as a sign of affection.

The surgeries were taking a toll on Kahlo's health, although around friends and visitors she still maintained her old cheerfulness. She did a lot of painting in those years of surgery and recuperation. *Still Life with Parrot,* done in 1951, shows a lush view of delicious-looking fruit, presided over by one of her pet parrots. Similar still lifes were *Light (Fruit of Life)* and *Long Live Life,* both painted in 1954, the year of her death. They are full of color and the bursting promise of life. That same year, she painted herself in a deep-red shawl next to a portrait of Stalin. Her brushstrokes were no longer as sure, but she continued working. Another self-portrait at that time shows a sketched image of a face on her forehead. In those later self-portraits, Kahlo began to decorate her forehead with symbols of thought.

In *Self-Portrait with Ixcuintle Dog and Sun,* she brings together the beloved elements of her life: Rivera, a pet dog, herself as a young woman, and the land of Mexico, bathed in golden sunlight.

Preparations began in 1953 for Kahlo's first one-woman show in her native land. It would be a retrospective of her work at the National Institute of Fine Arts. But the planning dragged on, and Rivera began to wonder if she would live long enough to attend. A friend, Lola Alvarez Bravo, came to the rescue. She offered to show the paintings at her large Galeria de Arte Contemporaneo. Rivera made the arrangements, and Kahlo chipped in by making the invitations.

When the show opened in April 1953, it seemed doubtful that Kahlo would be able to attend. By then, she was bedridden and practically surviving on painkillers. But Kahlo wasn't

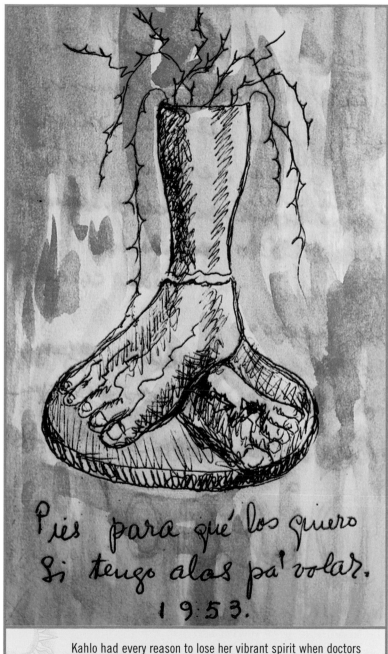

Pies para qué los quiero
Si tengo alas pa' volar.
1 9 5 3.

Kahlo had every reason to lose her vibrant spirit when doctors amputated her right leg in 1953. Instead, she was determined to enjoy life to the end, as referenced in this diary drawing of her severed leg with the words, "Feet, why do I want them if I have wings to fly?"

dead yet. She arrived at the show in an ambulance with a police motorcycle escort, sirens wailing. Her canopied bed had been brought from her home and installed in the middle of the gallery. An informal receiving line was set up, and each guest came up to her bed to greet her. It was certainly a unique moment in the history of art.

Kahlo told a reporter from *Time* magazine, "I am not sick. I am broken. But I am happy to be alive as long as I can paint."

The next month, Kahlo was hospitalized again. This time doctors had to amputate her right leg below the knee because of a gangrenous condition. Kahlo spent three months in the hospital. Typical of her, she made light of her condition to visiting friends. In fact, she drew a picture of her severed leg in her diary and wrote these words, "Pies para qué los quiero, si tengo alas pa' volar?" (Feet, why do I want them if I have wings to fly?)

But Kahlo began to think seriously of suicide. "They have given me centuries of torture and at moments I almost lost my reason," she wrote in her diary in February 1954. "I keep on wanting to kill myself. Diego is what keeps me from it through my vain idea that he would miss me. He has told me that and I believe it. But never in my life have I suffered more. I will wait a while . . ."

But it's not certain that she was willing to wait. She was hospitalized in April and May, possibly after suicide attempts.

Even though she had left the Communist Party after her husband had been expelled, Kahlo rejoined the party in 1952. She renounced her Trotskyite beliefs and embraced Stalin. Stalin, who governed the Soviet Union with an iron fist for 30 years, died the following year, but not before he ordered the execution of 19 Jewish activists for an imagined "Zionist conspiracy." (Zionism was the movement that inspired Jews to return to their homeland in Israel.) Writing in the *Washington Monthly* magazine, the journalist Stephanie Mencimer noted in a 2002 magazine article that Kahlo's embrace of Communism (particularly under Stalin), "led her to embrace some unfor-givable political positions."

As part of her new dedication to Communism, Kahlo painted *Marxism Will Give Health to the Sick* in 1954. She left behind an unfinished portrait of Stalin. By then, Kahlo was clearly dying. But she had to make one more political statement.

9

Long
Live Life!

Kahlo's final days were a mixture of sweetness, anger, and nastiness. As a former nurse, Judith Ferreto, put it, "During those days, she was going down rapidly." Ferreto added, "I think that she foresaw that she was going down and down."

Kahlo and Ferreto had a fight one day. Kahlo thought the nurse was bossing her around in her own home. She was very touchy and irritable at times. For instance, she no longer wanted children to visit, even though she had loved her nieces and nephews. "After the amputation, she hated children," Ferreto said. "The operation destroyed a personality. She loved life, she really loved life, but it was completely different after they amputated her leg."

Rivera himself was upset by Kahlo's behavior. Raquel Tibol, an art critic and longtime friend, recalled that once, when Kahlo was very sick and lay in a drugged state upstairs, Rivera arrived at the house and tried to eat lunch.

"He had come home to eat, but he didn't want to eat," Tibol said. "He began to cry like a child, and he said, 'If I were brave, I would kill her. I cannot stand to see her suffer so.' He cried like a child, cried and cried."

On another occasion, Kahlo threw a bottle of water at Rivera. He managed to duck out of the way. The sound of the breaking glass took the anger out of her. "Why did I do it?" she asked, crying. "Tell me, why did I do it? If I continue like this, I would prefer to die."

At other times, when Rivera had been away working and returned, Kahlo would say, "My child, where have you been, my child?" in a soft, loving voice.

Kahlo became a serious drug addict and got Rivera and others to buy her drugs. Once she asked another friend to give her an injection. He asked where he was going to get the drug, and she pointed to a drawer in a bureau. He opened it and found "a box with thousands of vials of Demerol."

Oddly, at the end of June 1954, Kahlo's health seemed to improve. She began talking about plans for the future, even saying she wanted to adopt a child. She had been invited to the Soviet Union, but she said she wouldn't go without Rivera. He had been ousted from the Communist Party and had not been readmitted even though he had asked to be.

Kahlo was looking forward to the silver wedding anniversary with Rivera on August 21. She planned a great Mexican fiesta and urged her friends to bring lots of people.

Meanwhile, on July 2, she disobeyed her doctors and left her bed to join an anti-American demonstration organized by the Communist Party in Mexico City. The event was to protest the removal of Guatemala's liberal president Jacobo Arbenz and the suspected involvement of the American Central Intelligence Agency (CIA) in replacing him with the reactionary General Castillo Armas. About 10,000 people showed up, and Kahlo was the star of the show. Rivera pushed her in her wheelchair through the crowds, and people fell in line behind them. Photographs show her looking wan and weak but bravely holding a banner in one hand and making a fist with the other. She had covered her head with a kerchief and she was not her usual jaunty self, but the rings on the fingers of her clenched fist glittered in the light of that gray, rainy day. Kahlo sat in her wheelchair for four hours, joining in the cry, "*Gringos asesinos, fuera!*" (Yankee assassins, get out!). She had been suffering with pneumonia, and being out in that damp weather for so long took a toll on her.

LAST BIRTHDAY PARTY

July 6 was Kahlo's forty-seventh birthday. She insisted on a celebration, and her friends gathered in the Casa Azul for the party. It was to be her last.

A hundred people came for her birthday celebration. She got dressed and made up her face. She was carried downstairs to the dining room where she greeted her friends. They ate a lunch of Mexican delicacies, and Kahlo seemed cheerful. Later, she was carried back upstairs and placed in her bed. She continued to talk to friends until late at night. She was not afraid of death. However, she had a dread of lying in her coffin and being lowered into the ground. It was in that position that she had suffered so much in her life. So, the decision was made that she would be cremated.

The last pages of her diary contain drawings of skeletons in costumes and strange, winged, female creatures. She wrote, "Muertes en relajo" (the dead having a fling). "We look for calm or 'peace,' because we anticipate death, since we die every moment," she wrote. The final drawing is of a dark angel rising into the sky. Accompanying it are the words, "Espero alegre la salida—y espero no volver jamas. Frida." (I hope for a happy exit and I hope never to come back.)

When Kahlo's old school friend and lawyer Manuel Gonzalez Ramirez visited her, he said they talked openly about her death, "because Frida was not afraid of it."

The day before she died, she told her nurse that she felt better. She said she had no pain. Rivera visited her in the

Kahlo and Rivera pose on the patio of the Casa Azul. Despite her weak condition, Kahlo insisted on hosting a large party for her forty-seventh birthday. She died just seven days later.

afternoon, and she started giving him advice. Kahlo warned him, "If you want your life to be aimless as a kite, just blown about by the wind, then that's the way it would be." Rivera told the nurse he would give her sleeping pills. "Frida usually put a bunch in her mouth all at once," the nurse said. "She was supposed to take only seven, so I told Señor Diego that, and I counted the pills that were in the jar."

Kahlo gave Rivera a ring she had hidden away as an anniversary present. Rivera said he asked Kahlo why she was giving him the ring so early, and she replied, "Because I feel I am going to leave you very soon."

"I sat beside her bed until 2:30 in the morning," Rivera said. Then he left her to go to his San Angel studio. When he returned in the morning, the nurse told him of the pain Kahlo had suffered in the night: "At four o'clock she complained of severe discomfort. When a doctor arrived at daybreak, he found that she had died a short time before of an embolism [clot] of the lungs."

"When I went into her room to look at her," Rivera wrote, "her face was tranquil and seemed more beautiful than ever."

Her nurse said she counted the sleeping pills and found that 11 were gone. Had Kahlo deliberately taken an overdose? Had she taken them accidentally? There was considerable speculation about the cause of her death. But her doctor insisted the cause was the embolism.

As for Rivera, those present said he turned old immediately. He locked himself in the bedroom and refused to see anyone as crowds of friends arrived at the Casa Azul. Later, he told his assistant, Emmy Lou Packard, "I had no idea I was going to miss her so much."

It was July 13, 1954. Rain was falling, wetting the beautiful garden of the Casa Azul that Kahlo loved so much and would never see again.

THE RIGHT ARTIST FOR THE RIGHT TIME

It almost seemed that Frida Kahlo's spirit was reluctant to leave her body. When a friend, Olga Campos, bent down to kiss her, she screamed when she thought she saw Kahlo's skin react with goose bumps. Then Rivera claimed he saw her hair stand on end and called the doctor.

"We're not entirely sure that she's really dead," he said. But he was convinced when the doctor opened a vein and no blood flowed.

More than 600 people came to mourn Kahlo's death. Among the honor guard was former Mexican president Lazaro Cardenas. The mourners walked solemnly in the rain behind the hearse carrying her body, which was dressed in her favorite Tehuana costume and bedecked with her spectacular jewelry, to the Palace of Fine Arts. There, Frida Kahlo lay in state while mourners passed her coffin.

Something of a scandal erupted when a former art student, Arturo Garcia Bustos, draped a Communist flag over her coffin. Andres Iduarte, who had known Kahlo in her school days and was now director of the Palace of Fine Arts, had asked Rivera not to turn the funeral into a political demonstration. Rivera had agreed, but he refused to have the flag removed. Iduarte was later fired over the incident.

The body was driven slowly through the gray drizzle along the Avenida Juarez to the Pantheon Civil de Delores, the municipal cemetery, for cremation. When Kahlo's body was being wheeled into the flames at the crematorium, it suddenly sat upright. Her hair, in flames, glowed like a wreath around her head. Witnesses screamed. But then the body fell back down. To some, it seemed that Kahlo's spirit was still strong enough, even in death, to make a final statement in favor of life. After all, her last painting, a still life, carried the inscription, "Viva la vida!" (Long live life!). Her friends and family sang hymns and her favorite Mexican songs as the fire consumed the earthly remains of one of Mexico's most treasured artists.

Rivera gathered Kahlo's ashes in a red silk scarf and placed them in a cedar box. He took them to the Casa Azul in Coyoacán, where they are on display today in a pre-Columbian urn. Despite all the pain he had given Kahlo, Rivera was genuinely devastated by her death. He looked pale and drawn at the funeral and never really regained his old flash. One consolation was that he was readmitted to the Communist Party as a reward for refusing to have its flag removed from Kahlo's coffin.

"The most tragic day of my life was 13 July 1954," he wrote in his autobiography. "I had lost my beloved Frida forever. Too late now, I realized that the most wonderful part of my life had been my love for Frida." He later told a friend, "Numerous critics in various countries have characterized Frida Kahlo's work as being the most vigorously rooted in Mexican folk art of all the Moderns. That's what I think, too." He added that her work "represents one of the most powerful and truthful human documents of our times. It will be of inestimable value for future generations."

Kahlo's home is open to visitors today. Rivera gave it to the Mexican people in 1955, and it was formally opened in

"LOST ARCHIVE" OR FORGERY?

For fans of Frida Kahlo, it was a seemingly monumental discovery—a collection of the artist's paintings, drawings, letters, diary entries, and other items previously unseen by the public. According to the *Art Newspaper*, the items are the focus of an illustrated book published in 2009. The book's publisher calls the subject matter "an astonishing lost archive of one of the twentieth century's most revered artists . . . full of ardent desires, seething fury, and outrageous humor." But a group of prominent Kahlo scholars sees it altogether differently: they say the collection is fake.

"In my view the publishers have been the victims of a gigantic hoax," says the New York–based art dealer Mary-Anne Martin, who has bought and sold numerous Kahlo paintings. "The perpetrators have constructed all these letters, poems, drawings and recipes, using Frida's biography and her published letters as a roadmap," she tells the *Art Newspaper*. "The drawings are badly done, the writing infantile, the content crude; the anatomy drawings look like something from a butcher shop instruction book. The paintings are 'pastiches,' composites based on published works."

1958. The tall windows facing the street are still bricked in from Trotsky's visit. The grotesque Judas figures that Kahlo liked guard the door. The house also contains many of her own paintings, as well as paintings by Rivera and others that she had purchased over the years. The rest of the house remains as it was in her lifetime, still cluttered with her photos, dolls, toys, and the other souvenirs with which she liked to surround herself. In her upstairs studio is an unfinished portrait of Joseph Stalin. From the hallway through an open door is a view of her cherished garden.

On the first anniversary of Kahlo's death, Rivera painted a smiling portrait of her with the inscription, "For the star of

The items belong to a couple who own an antique store in the Mexican town of San Miguel de Allende. The couple reportedly obtained them through a lawyer, who acquired them from a woodcarver, who allegedly received them from Kahlo herself.

Despite skepticism from Kahlo experts including Hayden Herrera and Salomon Grimberg, who coauthored Kahlo's *catalogue raisonné*, or official catalogue of published artworks, the book's publisher still went ahead with the book. The Princeton Architectural Press defends itself in an official statement appearing in the *Art Newspaper*: "These doubts are explored directly in the book, including a lengthy interview with the owners of the store and collection, the Noyola family, who believe, based on analyses by a chemical engineer and a graphologist, as well as interviews with members of the Kahlo family and some of her followers and students, that the materials in the cases are legitimate." Grimberg, on the other hand, didn't mince words when speaking on the topic to a group of reporters: "I have over 40 years of looking at the works of Frida and I can say that this is grotesque and vulgar."

The Communist Party flag is draped over Frida Kahlo's casket at the Mexican Palace of Fine Arts, where more than 600 mourners came to pay their last respects. The flag's presence caused a scandal, but Rivera refused to remove it.

my eyes, Fridita, who is still mine, 13 July 1955, Diego." Later that month, on July 29, Rivera married the publisher Emma Hurtado. But his new wife, as charming and beautiful as she was, was certainly no Frida Kahlo. It's unlikely that Rivera ever recovered from the death of the woman he had treated so insensitively for so many years.

Shortly after his marriage to Hurtado, Rivera went to the Soviet Union for cobalt treatments for prostate cancer. He continued to paint, both in Moscow and back in Mexico. Three years after Frida Kahlo's death, Rivera died of a heart attack in his San Angel studio on November 24, 1957. In February 2002, a large exhibition at Washington's National Museum of Women in the Arts featured Kahlo's paintings, along with those of Georgia O'Keeffe and Emily Carr. More than 28,000 people attended, and it was believed that Kahlo's works were the major attraction. Visitors left with tote bags full of Kahlo memorabilia, her unsmiling image on everything from watches to computer mouse pads.

As Gregorio Luke, director of the Museum of Latin American Art in California, said of Kahlo's recent popularity: "Frida Kahlo has been the right artist for the right time."

Chronology

1907 Born Magdalena Carmen Frida Kahlo y Calderón on July 6 in the Casa Azul in Coyoacán, Mexico, the third of Matilde Calderón and Guillermo Kahlo's four daughters.

1910 The Mexican Revolution begins. Kahlo will claim to be born during this year so that the year of her birth will coincide with the birth of the revolution.

1913 Contracts polio, permanently affecting her right leg.

1922 Enters the National Preparatory School, becomes member of mischief-making Cachuchas; teases Diego Rivera, who is painting a mural, *Creation,* at the school. Tells schoolmates she wants to have his baby.

1925 Permanently injured in a streetcar accident in Mexico City. Begins painting, using easel and mirror set up over her bed by her mother.

1928 Meets Diego Rivera again; asks him to look at her paintings.

1907
Born Magdalena Carmen Frida Kahlo y Calderón on July 6 in the Casa Azul in Coyoacán, Mexico, the third of Matilde Calderón and Guillermo Kahlo's four daughters

1922
Teases Diego Rivera, who is painting a mural at the school. Tells schoolmates she wants to have his baby

1929
Marries Rivera on August 21

1937
Begins an affair with Trotsky

1907

1937

1913
Contracts polio, permanently affecting her right leg

1925
Permanently injured in a streetcar accident in Mexico City. Begins painting, using easel and mirror set up over her bed by her mother

1935
Moves out of the house and takes an apartment, travels to New York with friends, returns, and reconciles with Rivera

1929 Marries Rivera on August 21.

1930 Goes to San Francisco, where Rivera has commissions to paint two murals. She is hospitalized with a problem with her foot.

1932 Goes with Rivera to Detroit, where Rivera has commissions to paint murals. Kahlo is hospitalized for a miscarriage. Her mother dies.

1933 Returns with Rivera to New York, where Rivera is commissioned by Nelson Rockefeller to paint a mural at the RCA Building.

1934 Back in Mexico, the married couple lives in a double house linked by a bridge in San Angel. Rivera begins an affair with Frida's younger sister, Cristina.

1935 Moves out of the house and takes an apartment, travels to New York with friends, returns, and reconciles with Rivera.

1939
The Louvre buys painting *The Frame*.
Divorces Rivera

1942
Self-Portrait with Braid shown at the Museum of Modern Art's Twentieth-Century Portraits with Ray Bar

1953
Kahlo's only individual exhibition in Mexico is held at the Galeria de Arte Contemporaneo

1938

1954

1938
First one-person exhibit runs at the Julien Levy Gallery in New York

1940
The Two Fridas and *The Wounded Table* are included in the International Surrealism Exhibition at the Gallery of Mexican Art

1950
Hospitalized for nine months for recurring spinal problems

1954
Dies on July 13

1937 Leon Trotsky and his wife arrive in Mexico and live in Casa Azul in hiding. Kahlo begins an affair with Trotsky.

1938 Edward G. Robinson buys four of Kahlo's paintings; her first one-person exhibit runs at the Julien Levy Gallery in New York.

1939 The Louvre buys painting *The Frame.* Divorces Rivera.

1940 *The Two Fridas* and *The Wounded Table* are included in the International Surrealism Exhibition at the Gallery of Mexican Art. Leon Trotsky is murdered by an agent of Joseph Stalin. Kahlo and Rivera remarry.

1942 Father dies; Kahlo moves to the Casa Azul in Coyoacán. *Self-Portrait with Braid* shown at the Museum of Modern Art's Twentieth-Century Portraits.

1943 Paintings are exhibited at a group show, A Century of the Portrait in Mexico (1830–1942) at the Benjamin Franklin Library, Mexico City; in Mexican Art Today at the Philadelphia Museum of Art; and at Peggy Guggenheim's Art of This Century Gallery in New York. Begins teaching at the Ministry of Public Education's School of Painting and Sculpture, La Esmeralda.

1946 Surgery performed on Kahlo's spine.

1947 *Self-Portrait as a Tehuana (Diego in My Thoughts)* exhibited in Forty-Five Self-Portraits by Mexican Painters from XVIII to the XX Centuries at the National Institute of Fine Arts in Mexico City.

1949 *The Love Embrace of the Universe, the Earth (Mexico), Me, Diego and Mr. Xolotl,* is exhibited at the inaugural exhibition of the Salon de la Plastica Mexicana.

1950 Hospitalized for nine months for recurring spinal problems.

1953 Kahlo's only individual exhibition in Mexico is held at the Galeria de Arte Contemporaneo. She attends, although she has to greet guests lying in bed in the gallery.

1954   Critically ill with bronchial pneumonia, but takes part in an anti-American demonstration over Guatemala on July 2. Dies on July 13.

1957   Diego Rivera dies.

1958   The Casa Azul is opened to the public as the Frida Kahlo Museum.

1983   The first full-length biography of Kahlo, written by Hayden Herrera, is published.

2002   The major motion picture *Frida* and several books on Kahlo's life and art are released.

Bibliography

Alcantara, Isabel, and Sandra Egnoff. *Frida Kahlo and Diego Rivera.* Munich, London, New York: Prestel Verlag, 1999.

Burrus, Christina. *Frida Kahlo: Painting Her Own Reality.* New York: Abrams, 2008.

Castro-Sethness, Maria A. "Frida Kahlo's Spiritual World: The Influence of Mexican Retablo and Ex-Voto Paintings on Her Art." *Woman's Art Journal* 25, no. 2 (Autumn 2004–Winter 2005): 21–24.

Cockroft, James. *Diego Rivera.* Philadelphia: Chelsea House Publishers, 1991.

Giese, Lucretia Hoover. "A Rare Crossing: Frida Kahlo and Luther Burbank." *American Art* 15, no. 1 (Spring 2005): 53–73.

Hardin, Terri. *Frida Kahlo: A Modern Master.* New York: Smithmark Publishers, 1997.

Herrera, Hayden. *Frida: A Biography of Frida Kahlo.* New York: Harper Perennial, 2002.

Kettenmann, Andrea. *Kahlo.* Köln, Germany: Taschen, 2000.

Mencimer, Stephanie. "The Trouble with Frida Kahlo." *Washington Monthly*, June 2002. Available online. URL: http://www.washingtonmonthly.com/features/2001/0206.mencimer.html.

Moore, Thomas. *The Soul's Religion.* New York: HarperCollins, 2002.

Mujica, Barbara. "Looking for Cultural Icons and Love." *Americas* (English Edition), Nov.–Dec. 2004. Available online. URL: http://findarticles.com/p/articles/mi_go2043/is_6_56/ai_n7463665/.

Ronnen, Meir. "Frida Kahlo's Father Wasn't Jewish After All." *Jerusalem Post*, April 20, 2006.

Rummel, Jack. *Frida Kahlo: A Spiritual Biography.* New York: Crossroad Publishing Co., 2000.

Sullivan, Edward J. *The Language of Objects in the Art of the Americas.* New Haven, Conn.: Yale University Press, 2007.

Tuchman, Phyllis. "Frida Kahlo." *Smithsonian Magazine*, November 2002.

Zamora, Martha. *Frida Kahlo: The Brush of Anguish.* San Francisco: Chronicle Books, 1990.

Further Reading

Casagrande, Louis B., and S.A. Johnson. *Focus on Mexico: Modern Life in an Ancient Land.* New York: Lerner, 1986.

Fisher, Leonard E. *Pyramid of the Sun, Pyramid of the Moon.* New York: Macmillan, 1988.

Herrera, Hayden. *Frida Kahlo: The Paintings.* New York: HarperCollins, 1991.

Kahlo, Frida. *The Diary of Frida Kahlo: An Intimate Self-Portrait.* New York: Abradale Press, 2002.

Kettenmann, Andrea. *Frida Kahlo: Pain and Passion.* New York: Taschen America, 2000.

Stein, R. Conrad. *Mexico.* New York: Children's Press, 1984.

Winter, Jonah, and Ana Juan. *Frida.* New York: Scholastic Press, 2002.

Web Sites

The Art History Network: Frida Kahlo
http://www.arthistory.net/artists/kahlo.html

Biography of Frida Kahlo (Keyword: Kahlo)
http://www.brain-juice.com

Carlos Pellicer
http://en.wikipedia.org/wiki/Carlos_Pellicer

Frida Kahlo and Contemporary Thoughts
http://www.fridakahlo.it

Frida Kahlo: Diego's Lover and Friend
http://www.fbuch.com/fridakahlo.htm

Frida Kahlo in the Florence Arquin Papers
http://www.archivesofamericanart.si.edu/htgmonth/hispanic/arquin.htm

Picture Credits

Index

About the Authors

John Morrison is a longtime Philadelphia newspaperman who has worked as a reporter, writer, and editor. He has had short stories and poetry published and has edited several novels for a Dell Publishing subsidiary.

Jamie Pietras is a writer and journalist who lives in New York City. He holds an M.F.A. in creative writing with a concentration in nonfiction from Columbia University.